DISCOVERING
DELIGHT

DISCOVERING
DELIGHT

31 Meditations on Loving God's Law

Glenda Mathes

Reformation Heritage Books
Grand Rapids, Michigan

Discovering Delight
© 2014 by Glenda Mathes

Reformation Heritage Books
2965 Leonard St. NE
Grand Rapids, MI 49525
616-977-0889 / Fax 616-285-3246
orders@heritagebooks.org
www.heritagebooks.org

Printed in the United States of America
14 15 16 17 18 19/10 9 8 7 6 5 4 3 2 1

Library of Congress Control Number: 2014951739

For additional Reformed literature, request a free book list from Reformation Heritage Books at the above regular or e-mail address.

CONTENTS

Contents

PREFACE

And I will delight myself in thy commandments, which I have loved.
—PSALM 119:47

The concept of loving law clashes in modern ears like crashing cymbals. Today's Christians don't want to read about law. They want to revel in gospel and grace. But the Bible clearly links law with love. If you question this, read Psalm 119, a long psalm that often gets short shrift.

As the longest chapter of the Bible, it seems too much to memorize or read during devotions. Because it so often mentions God's law, we may think of it as legalistic, boring, or repetitive. This intricately constructed acrostic poem, however, radiates joy for God's Word and generates delight in His timeless promises. Hebrew readers studying it in its original language may notice poetical devices that are lost to readers of English versions, but love for God's Word shines through in any language.

While at least one of eight Hebrew words for God's law appears in nearly every one of the psalm's 176 verses, forms of "I" and "you" appear even more frequently. That's because Psalm 119 is more than a carefully crafted poem praising God's Word. It is the passionate prayer of an individual in authentic communion with God. The psalmist is a person very much like you and me—he struggles with sin and suffering, cries for divine help, and rejoices in the God who hears and answers prayer.

Psalm 119's praise of God and His Word is not isolated. Other psalms, Old Testament passages, and New Testament texts specifically extol God's law and encourage believers to love the written as well as the living Word.

Before examining each of Psalm 119's twenty-two sections, *Discovering Delight: 31 Meditations on Loving God's Law* reflects on five law-exalting poems that appear earlier in the Psalter (1, 19, 37, 40, 112). Then, *Discovering Delight* explores two passages from the prophets (Isaiah 58, Jeremiah 15) and two New Testament texts (Romans 7, Revelation 19) that express sensory delight in the Word of God.

I want to express my appreciation to Dr. Peter J. Wallace, whose online sermons on Psalm 119 (www.peterwallace .org/sermons.htm) I discovered when this manuscript was nearly complete. His explanations—especially of Hebrew words and their placement in the text—expanded my understanding and confirmed much of what I had written. His sermons affirmed my view of the psalm's beauty as well as its practicality. I also wish to express my sincere appreciation to Rev. Mark Vander Hart, associate professor of Old Testament studies at Mid-America Reformed Seminary, whose early explanations regarding the Hebrew alphabet and the character of God's covenant love guided my reflections.

Unless otherwise noted, Scripture quotations are from the King James Version of the Bible. Occasional quotations appear from the Heidelberg Catechism, which is a highly personal set of questions and answers exploring the biblical comfort of belonging to Christ. This catechism, the Belgic

Confession (also mentioned in these meditations), and the Canons of Dort were written in the early years following the Protestant Reformation to help people understand scriptural truth and unite the fledgling Protestant churches on the European Continent. These documents are known as the Three Forms of Unity and are embraced by Reformed churches. The Westminster Shorter Catechism—also mentioned in these meditations—is a simplified version of the Westminster Larger Catechism, both of which originated with the Westminster Confession during seventeenth-century English Puritanism. The Westminster Standards are utilized by Presbyterian churches.

The subject of loving God's law attracted me because I needed to know what the Bible says about delight. It is a lesson I still study. As with so many things, the more I learn, the more I see how much I have yet to learn.

May God's Spirit fill your heart with joy and peace as you read these meditations. May they whet your appetite for feasting on God's written and living Word!

—Glenda Mathes

FRUITFUL TREE

1

Scripture Reading: Psalm 1

But his delight is in the law of the LORD; and in his law doth he meditate day and night.

—PSALM 1:2

The first song in the Psalter puts readers into meditation mode, comparing the believer to a fruitful tree and stressing how the blessed person delights in the Lord's law. The psalm's first verse describes the man (or woman) who is blessed by expressing the negatives of three actions. He or she does not walk in the counsel of the ungodly, does not stand in the way of sinners, and does not sit in the seat of the scornful. Walking, standing, and sitting represent three different levels of action. Walking is the most active physically, but sitting could very well be the most active mentally.

The blessed person doesn't take part in ungodly activities or implement ungodly counsel. While Christians may develop relationships with unbelievers, especially for the purpose of evangelism, they don't stand with them in sinful or fruitless pursuits. And they don't sit in on plans with people who scorn God's name and Word.

Blessing comes to the person who makes conscious and committed efforts to avoid ill-advised actions, sinful philosophies, and scornful attitudes. But blessing derives from more than merely avoiding bad behaviors. Verse 2 tells us that actively meditating on God's law brings blessing and delight. The godly person loves God's Word so much that he or she meditates on it day and night.

Reading Scripture early in the morning as the first fruits of your day is a good start. Meditating on God's Word again in the evening is even better. But this verse encompasses much more than a command for daily and nightly personal devotions. It's about loving God's law so intensely that you long to spend time reveling in it. Your mind and heart become so steeped in Scripture that portions of the Word saturate your thoughts and accompany your daily activities. Meditating day and night is an attitude as well as an action.

In lovely imagery, Psalm 1:3 describes the blessed person as a firmly rooted, fruitful tree with unwithered leaves. Its roots reach toward life-giving rivers, drinking deeply of living waters. At the proper time it brings forth sound fruit. It is full of lustrous green leaves, free from pest or blight. The image of a tree budding in the spring, bursting with full foliage in the summer, and bearing ripe fruit in the fall effectively pictures the believer performing righteous deeds through the progression of time and the process of personal sanctification.

The believer-as-tree simile occurs repeatedly in Scripture. Jeremiah 17:8 echoes Psalm 1:3 in remarkably similar words: "For he shall be as a tree planted by the waters, and that spreadeth out her roots by the river, and shall not see when heat cometh, but her leaf shall be green; and shall not be careful in the year of drought, neither shall cease from yielding fruit" (Jer. 17:8). Despite heat and drought, this believer tree will produce fruit and enjoy peace. Christians who drink deeply of God's living waters will bear the fruit of righteousness and experience peace that passes understanding, even during times of scorching physical adversity or arid spiritual drought.

Ezekiel uses similar language when describing the trees he sees in a vision:

> And by the river upon the bank thereof, on this side and on that side, shall grow all trees for meat, whose leaf shall not fade, neither shall the fruit thereof be consumed: it shall bring forth new fruit according to his months, because their waters they issued out of the sanctuary: and the fruit thereof shall be for meat, and the leaf thereof for medicine. (Ezek. 47:12)

These trees drink of water that issues from God's holy sanctuary. Although their fruit will be used for food, it will not disappear; the leaf will not fade despite being used for healing. Doesn't this imagery remind you of the Tree of Life in the garden of Eden (Gen. 2:9) and still more of the final Tree of Life from which believers will eat in the superior paradise (Rev. 2:7)? Just as the leaves of the tree in Ezekiel's vision would become medicine, the leaves of the definitive Tree of Life will be for the healing of the nations (Rev. 22:2).

To say that the blessed person prospers in all things doesn't mean that every believer will experience business success, enjoy physical health, and live within a happy family. God may allow a Christian to struggle for decades under financial adversity, to suffer for much of life from chronic pain and fatigue, or to grieve for years the heartache of a wayward child. Believers sometimes experience worldly prosperity, but often they do not. True prosperity is not found in the things of this world, but in the things of the eternal realm. All that is done for Christ counts as success in His kingdom. And believers prosper eternally because their future is secure in Christ.

This isn't true for the wicked. The future of the ungodly is far from secure. Verse 4 shows that in contrast to the sturdy believer tree, firmly rooted beside refreshing streams, unbelievers are like bits of grain husks blown into oblivion by the blustery wind.

The ungodly will not be able to stand before the judgment seat of Christ or in the great and final gathering of the righteous (v. 5). They will crumple under the scrutiny of God's final judgment. And those who persist in sin will have no place in the ultimate and unified congregation of the church triumphant.

The way of the wicked will perish, but God knows the way of the righteous (v. 6). He sees your struggle right now. He knows what will happen to you today, this week, this month, and every year for the rest of your life. He will watch over your every step in this temporal life and in all aspects of your eternal future. Because of Christ's finished work, believers will stand without faltering before His judgment. They will join the righteous throng that enters the city gates and partakes of the tree of life (Rev. 22:14).

As you begin this devotional of meditating on God's Word, may His Spirit fill your heart with joy in your Lord and love for His delightful law.

Questions for Reflection

How might I be walking, standing, or sitting in ways that compromise my Christian faith?

What is my attitude about God's Word and meditating on it?

What specific steps can I take to become more like a believer tree?

2

ELEGANT BOOK

Scripture Reading: Psalm 19

The heavens declare the glory of God; and the firmament sheweth his handywork.

—PSALM 19:1

Since psalms are Hebrew poetry, we need to read them differently from the historical portions of Scripture. Rather than viewing them as subsequent chapters in a narrative, we must see the book of Psalms as a series of poetical reflections. A poem often moves suddenly from one topic to another, and few psalms contain shifts that seem more abrupt than Psalm 19. The first six verses speak in vivid imagery about God's world, but verse 7 switches into a lovely ode extolling God's Word. Is this shift as illogical as it might initially appear?

Not when we consider that God reveals Himself in two ways: general revelation and special revelation—His world and His Word. Article 2 of the Belgic Confession beautifully expresses biblical truth regarding the two ways God reveals Himself:

> We know Him by two means: First, by the creation, preservation, and government of the universe; which is before

our eyes as a most elegant book, wherein all creatures, great and small, are as so many characters leading us to *see clearly the invisible things of God*, even *his everlasting power and divinity*, as the apostle Paul says (Romans 1:20). All which things are sufficient to convince men and leave them without excuse. Second, He makes Himself more clearly and fully known to us by His holy and divine Word, that is to say, as far as is necessary for us to know in this life, to His glory and our salvation.

This quote from the Belgic Confession helps us see how Psalm 19, despite the apparent sudden shift in content, is one unified whole extolling God's general as well as His special revelation. The Confession's comparison of the created cosmos to "a most elegant book" strengthens our understanding of Psalm 19's unity. The open tome of creation leads us to seek further understanding by opening the Word of God. The Confession's language delightfully reflects the literary tone of Psalm 19's first six verses.

God created the sun, moon, and stars. We know from Genesis 1:14 that He set them in the heavens as signs. Day after day and night after night, they clearly testify to God's creative power and continual order. Psalm 19 confirms that the witness of the heavenly bodies spans the whole earth and can be understood in any language.

God's general revelation transcends the confusion brought about at the Tower of Babel. God's works declare His glory in neon lights that no one can ignore. The gospel of a good and intelligent Creator who delights in orderly variety and inspiring beauty is nightly written in bright points of light punctuating the dark heavens and daily inscribed in warm beams of sunshine radiating from a blue sky.

Psalm 19 uses the literary device of simile to depict the sun as a resplendent bridegroom eagerly leaving his chamber. Can't you imagine a beaming young Israelite man, clothed in richly decorated garments, parting the canvas hangings of a tent to go forward to meet his betrothed? Scripture frequently portrays the relationship of Christ to His church like that of a groom to his bride. God initiated His covenant relationship with the church. Christ is the head of the church now and will come for His bride one day. Perhaps that's why in traditional Christian ceremonies, the first member of the wedding party to enter is the groom.

With another simile, Psalm 19 compares the sun in its circuit to a strong man joyfully running a race. Moms attending track meets or dads watching sports shows have seen an exultant runner crossing the finish line. Anyone can envision how a runner throws every part of his being into that final push and thrusts his arms high in ecstatic elation as he breaks the red ribbon. These literary images give us a glimpse of how the sun crowns God's magnificent creation and how it reflects His authority, beauty, strength, and joy.

Creation also shows us God's omnipresence and omniscience. Verse 6 tells us that the sun goes from one end of the heaven to the other and nothing is hid from its heat. How much more is the world exposed under God's eye! He is everywhere present—He sees and knows all things. Though the sun appears to move in a circuit around the earth, we know that the earth actually orbits the sun. Isn't this a bit like the way we tend to think of God? I am often so self-centered that, without even realizing it, I think of myself as the center of the universe, as if God and all His benefits revolve around me. In reality I am only a small speck in space, a tiny creature in a vast cosmos whose entire existence revolves around its Creator God.

Following the lovely imagery about celestial bodies that act as a most elegant book and declare the glory of God, Psalm 19 shifts into a paean praising God's law. As we noted earlier, this change seems less sudden if we see the psalmist moving from praising God's general revelation to extolling His special revelation.

The union may be even more organic than we think. Although we need God's written Word to know and understand His salvation plan, the heavens direct our thoughts and praise to God, which leads us to seek His will from His Word.

Verses 7 through 9 of Psalm 19 describe God's law in eloquent language:

> The law of the LORD is perfect, converting the soul: the testimony of the LORD is sure, making wise the simple. The statutes of the LORD are right, rejoicing the heart: the commandment of the LORD is pure, enlightening the eyes. The fear of the LORD is clean, enduring for ever: the judgments of the LORD are true and righteous altogether.

Notice all the descriptors? The law of the Lord is perfect, sure, right, pure, clean, and righteous. It is the ultimate ideal. Note also the many present participles, "ing" verbs, in this section. What is the law doing? It is converting the soul, making wise the simple, rejoicing the heart, enlightening the eyes, and enduring forever. Such action verb phrases vibrantly depict God's law as living and active (see also Heb. 4:12).

After the psalmist makes God's Word come alive, he exalts its value as better treasure than much fine gold. It surpasses a sunken chest filled with gold doubloons. It out-shines the British crown jewels. It exceeds Bill Gates's bank account. Who wouldn't want such remarkable wealth?

God's Word is more than valuable; it is sweet, sweeter than golden honey, fresh from the comb, dripping off a warm homemade biscuit. We should crave God's mouth-watering words and delight in them more than the most delicious food.

From verse 11, we learn that Scripture warns and rewards us. It alerts us to ways we tend to sin. It also shows that keeping God's commandments leads to a sense of peace and a feeling of joy. As we obey, we increasingly delight in doing God's will.

As the psalmist turns to personal petitions, he acknowl-edges that we all overlook our own sins. He asks God to cleanse him from "secret faults" (v. 12), which could include the sins he hides from others as well as the sins he himself fails to see. He pleads with God to keep him from "pre-sumptuous sins" so that they don't gain "dominion" in his life (v. 13). These presumptuous sins could be willful sins—when we really know that what we're doing is not right, but we do it anyway. They could also be the presumption that God will forgive us or that we're not so bad. Such a sin might be assuming we're saved, but producing hypocritical or legalistic fruit that rots from the inside out. These atti-tudes lead to sinful behaviors that gain mastery over us. In contrast, the humble heart produces righteous fruit. Even though we're all sinners, God sees believers as upright and innocent because of Christ's atonement.

The final verse of Psalm 19 is a personal favorite that is frequently in my mind: "Let the words of my mouth, and the meditation of my heart, be acceptable in thy sight, O LORD, my strength, and my redeemer" (v. 14). Here is a prayer that is appropriate before every church function, family reunion, or friendly get-together. It is just as important to pray before meeting a friend for coffee as prior to confronting someone about a sin. It is a wonderful prayer while you are driving somewhere and mulling over what you'll say when you get there. But it is also great as what I call a "Nehemiah prayer": the kind of quick, split-second prayer for guidance that Nehemiah cast up to the Lord before answering King Artaxerxes's question (Neh. 2:4). This is a prayer for God to guide everything I think, do, and say and to look on all my thoughts, actions, and words with His favor. Would God be pleased with the words that easily slip from my lips, the thoughts on which I relentlessly dwell, and the desires I cherish in my heart? This is a prayer worth engraving in the brain.

May this be your prayer wherever you are today and wherever the Lord leads you far into the future. May you view every part of God's creation as His most elegant book and daily immerse yourself in His written book. When we read the Bible, we increase our ability to recognize our sins, even the pride and other pet sins so stubbornly ingrained and deeply hidden in our hearts, and we desire more to live for God while increasingly delighting in His world and His Word.

Questions for Reflection

How does considering creation as a most elegant book expand my concept of God's character?

If I look deeply at my own heart, what stubborn sins do I hide from others and even from myself?

In what specific ways can I demonstrate to God and others my mastery over presumptuous sins?

3

HEART'S DESIRE

Scripture Reading: Psalm 37

Delight thyself also in the LORD: and he shall give thee the desires of thine heart.

—PSALM 37:4

What a lovely verse! Don't you want God to give you the desires of your heart? While it is wonderful to memorize precious passages and frequently repeat them to ourselves, we need to consider such verses in context. We may be surprised at how often our favorite texts are coupled with calls to repentance, obedience, or humility.

Psalm 37 is an acrostic poem, crafted according to the letters of the Hebrew alphabet. Knowing this increases our appreciation for the psalm's construction and the focus verse's context. Verse 4 contains one of Psalm 37's multiple references to the delight and blessing the righteous enjoy now and forever. But before listing any blessings, the psalm first tells us not to fret about evildoers, assuring us that their days are numbered. They will soon be mown down like grass and wither as the green herb. Since their iniquity is temporary, we shouldn't worry about their works and deeds or be envious of their prosperity and ease.

The verse immediately before our focus verse forcefully calls us, through the use of imperatives, to total trust and godly behavior: "Trust in the LORD, and do good; so shalt thou dwell in the land, and verily thou shalt be fed" (v. 3). In contrast to the evildoers' transience, those who trust in God and work for good will enjoy a place in the land and provision from God. While we sojourn on this earth, God provides homes for us to live in and food for us to eat; He allows us to dwell in security and peace.

The last clause of verse 3 has been translated and interpreted differently by various scholars. Some emphasize faith while others stress safety, sincerity, or truth. In his commentary on this verse, John Calvin bemoans how various interpreters have been led by personal ambition "to seek for something new" while "the true and natural meaning," which should have occurred to them at once, is "dwell in the land, that thou mayest enjoy it in sure and lasting repose." He believes the Hebrew signifies "truth or faith" and also "secure continuance for a long period."

As we trust the Lord and work for good within our spheres of influence, God calls us to enjoy the life He has given us and rest in His enduring protection. Even though trust and rest may seem to imply inaction, we're called to active engagement. We shouldn't withdraw from society or set our hope on heaven to the exclusion of our earthly responsibilities.

If we are trusting God, doing good, living an engaged life, and resting in the Lord, will it affect the desires of our hearts? Do you think our desires may become a little less self-focused and self-centered? Absolutely.

Verse 4 itself lists another precondition to God's granting heart desires: Delight also in the Lord. The "also" indicates that this is in addition to the previous requirements. Like the initial verbs in verse 3 ("trust," "do good"), "delight" is an imperative that conveys a command rather than a recommendation or suggestion.

Consider what it means to delight in the Lord. It includes loving Him wholeheartedly and serving Him willingly. It embraces wanting to spend time with Him in personal meditation and prayer. But it goes beyond that to enjoying God, which is as important as glorifying Him.

The Westminster Shorter Catechism defines our "chief end" as "to glorify God, and to enjoy him forever" (Q&A 1). Compare for a moment this idea of enjoying God to how you feel about the people you most love. A young man longs to spend every free minute with his fiancé. A grandmother rejoices to hug her grandson and marvels at his increasing conversational skills. A mother likes nothing better than when her adult children come over for Sunday lunch. A husband looks forward to coming home after a long day of work and relaxing with his wife. We all have obligations toward those we love, but we delight in our relationships when we move beyond responsibility to enjoyment. Delight in the Lord surpasses duty; it is an intense longing to be with Him and rest in His presence. The delighted heart overflows with joy, and as we rejoice in the Lord, our desires turn from self toward Him. We long for His will rather than our own. Delight directs desire.

The section following our focus verse also contains imperatives: *commit, trust, rest, wait, fret not, cease from anger, forsake wrath*, and, again, *fret not*. As we commit our way to God and trust Him, we are increasingly able to wait for Him to act. God brings resolution in His perfect time. It's hard to wait, especially when we are waiting for our hearts' desires. We often become impatient, so we run ahead of God's timetable with actions we think should be taken—and should be taken *now*!

But if we delight in the Lord while waiting on Him, our desire conforms to His will. Our righteousness and justice shine brighter as they reflect His. God also calls us to stop being angry, to forsake wrath, and *twice* to refrain from fretting. Why did God begin this psalm with the command not to fret and repeat it two more times in these verses? Perhaps because many people, like me, tend to fret. Verse 8 convicts me that my fretting tends toward evil. I can't expect God to grant heart desires or illumine godly righteousness unless I trust more and fret less.

Just as Psalm 37's first few verses contrasted the transience of the wicked with the permanence of the righteous, verses 9 through the end of the psalm contrast curses for the wicked with blessings for the righteous. Within this lengthy list of contrasts, we see frequent promises for believers, including these pearls: "But the meek shall inherit the earth; and shall delight themselves in the abundance of peace…. The steps of a good man are ordered by the LORD: and he delighteth in his way. Though he fall, he shall not be utterly cast down: for the LORD upholdeth him with his hand" (vv. 11, 23–24). God rewards the humble believer with the joy of place and peace. God guides those who delight in His way. Even when you fall, you won't land flat on your face. God holds your hand and lifts you up.

The psalm continues with comfort. Because of God's generosity to us, we should give freely to others, confident that God will not leave us destitute. He will never forsake us. If God's law remains in our hearts, our steps will not slip. God promises the man of peace a future and salvation. He is our stronghold and our refuge (vv. 25–40).

In this acrostic psalm, God calls us to trust totally in Him with humble hearts that want to serve Him and delight in Him. If we want God to grant our desires, we must examine the heart motives that drive those desires.

Questions for Reflection

What actions can I take today to do good while living an engaged life for God's glory?

How can I move beyond dutiful responsibility to a delightful relationship with the Lord?

If I genuinely examine my heart's motivations, what drives my desires?

4 IMPATIENCE INVERSION

Scripture Reading: Psalm 40

I delight to do thy will, O my God: yea, thy law is within my heart.

—PSALM 40:8

Most laments begin with restlessly crying to God, but end with patiently waiting on His will. Psalm 40 reverses that order. It begins with a patient wait and ends with an impatient plea. Almost exactly in the middle, our focus verse speaks of delighting to do God's will and keeping His Word within the heart.

David had experienced what he depicts as a life-threatening situation. He describes it as a horrible pit and a miry bog. But while he was in this terrible trouble, he prayed faithfully and waited patiently. God inclined His ear and heard David's cry. He set David's feet firmly on a solid rock so that he could walk with confidence (vv. 1–2).

We don't know how long David had to wait for God to answer. It may have been a crisis situation when minutes seemed like hours. It could have been a chronic condition that lasted literal years. However long David waited, he did so patiently.

God went beyond mere deliverance to reward David by filling his heart and mouth with creative praise. The new song that God gave David became a musical witness and the Holy Spirit's vehicle to bring many others to trust in the Lord (v. 3).

David then describes a person who is blessed by God. Blessing comes from trusting in God, turning from pride, and walking in truth (v. 4). God blesses His people in countless ways; His wonderful works and His loving thoughts toward His children are beyond compare. David will proclaim God's marvelous deeds, but they are more than any one person can recount (v. 5).

As we see in other texts (1 Sam. 15:22; Ps. 51:15; Prov. 21:3; Heb. 10:5–7), God does not delight in sacrifices and burnt offerings. He delights in ears that are open to hearing His Word (v. 6). God's Spirit opens ears to hear biblical truth and softens hearts to move beyond external religious practices to genuine personal piety.

All of this prefaces our focus verse and the one immediately before it: "Then said I, Lo, I come: in the volume of the book it is written of me, I delight to do thy will, O my God: yea, thy law is within my heart" (vv. 7–8).

After the Spirit opens our ears and softens our hearts, we offer ourselves to God willingly and cheerfully. When David mentions a book, he may be referring to his name written in God's Book of Life (Rev. 3:5; 21:27). As the king of Israel who foreshadowed Christ, David is also indicating how all Scripture points to Him, as He declared Himself to be the fulfillment of the law and prophets (Luke 24:27, 44). In too many texts to list—several of which this devotional explores—the psalmist also speaks of delighting to obey

God and holding His Word in his heart. David may have known and identified with one of these, which he repeats here. Whether David had in mind any or all of these things as he wrote these verses, it is clear that he rejoices in doing God's will and recalling His Word. He submits joyfully as a living sacrifice before God. He delights to do God's will in his life and to hide His law in his heart.

But David doesn't keep God's attributes hidden. Just as he records his verbal witness in verse 3, he confesses in verses 9 and 10 that he will publicly declare God's attributes, specifically His righteousness, faithfulness, salvation, loving-kindness, and truth. And he doesn't keep God's answers to prayer a secret; he freely shares with others the glad news of the many ways God has delivered him.

We see a shift in David's reflection as he pleads for God's continued mercy and preservation in verse 11. He describes a terrible battle that he wages externally and internally. Innumerable evils surround him while his own countless sins overwhelm him. His head bows and his heart fails (v. 12).

Psalm 40 concludes with petitions and imprecations that become increasingly urgent:

> Be pleased, O LORD, to deliver me: O LORD, make haste to help me.
>
> Let them be ashamed and confounded together that seek after my soul to destroy it; let them be driven backward and put to shame that wish me evil. Let them be desolate for a reward of their shame that say unto me, Aha, aha. Let all those that seek thee rejoice and be glad in thee: let such as love thy salvation say continually, the LORD be magnified.

But I am poor and needy; yet the Lord thinketh upon me: thou art my help and my deliverer; make no tarrying, O my God. (vv. 13–17)

If those verses sound familiar, it may be because you have recently read Psalm 70. The five verses of that short psalm almost exactly echo the above verses from Psalm 40. And they are not the only psalms that express a desire for God's speedy deliverance. Psalms 38, 71, and 141 all plead with God to "make haste" in helping the psalmist.

How should we view these seemingly impatient pleas? Although we know that we must wait patiently on God's will, these texts indicate that there are times when it's perfectly appropriate to ask God to act quickly. God knows and understands our human emotions, including our occasional impatience. When chronic cares or urgent crises overwhelm us, it is fitting to pray the words of these psalms. When persecutors surround us and rejoice in our pain, we certainly may pray for God to foil their plans. We can follow those requests with prayers for God's blessing on His people so that believers will be able to rejoice and be glad as they magnify God's name together. When we feel poor and needy, we can confess that God is our help and our deliverer. And David's words show us that we may add to any of these petitions a request for God not to delay, to hasten to our aid.

Nearly all of us will have times when we feel an urgent need for God's deliverance. Trauma or trouble turn our world upside down and invert our patience. But God didn't make us mechanical robots; He created us as multifaceted individuals who respond emotionally to crisis. During times of acute distress, we can pray God's own words as we plead with Him to "make haste" and deliver us.

Questions for Reflection

What "new song" has the Lord put in my mouth that I need to share with others?

In what ways might I be offering sacrifices without open ears and a soft heart?

How can I, and how can I help others, practice impatience properly?

DAWNING LIGHT

5

Scripture Reading: Psalm 112

Praise ye the LORD. Blessed is the man that feareth the LORD, that delighteth greatly in his commandments.
—PSALM 112:1

A long struggle during a dark time can seem like an endless night. Yet even in affliction we can delight in God and trust that His light will dawn.

We can hope for God's dawning light because that's what He promises in Psalm 112. Successive letters of the Hebrew alphabet begin each half verse of this acrostic psalm. That construction aided memorization when education was passed on primarily through oral tradition. One can imagine Jewish children learning their alphabet as they learned the manifold ways God blesses His people.

Like many psalms, Psalm 112 opens with a call to praise the Lord. But instead of continuing to praise God, it begins an extended beatitude. God blesses the person who fears Him and delights in His commandments.

Does it seem a bit odd to delight in commandments? We don't like to be told what to do. We don't want to be legalists, bound by rules and regulations. We prefer to think of ourselves as independent, free from commands and constraints. But if we truly love and honor God, we are neither legalists nor individualists. We humbly realize our complete dependence upon God's grace, and we joyfully delight in His will and His Word.

I like to envision children learning the words of this psalm because of its covenantal character. It assures believers of God's loving care for ensuing generations: "His seed shall be mighty upon earth: the generation of the upright shall be blessed. Wealth and riches shall be in his house: and his righteousness endureth for ever" (Ps. 112:2–3).

Our children may not lift heavy weights or win wrestling matches, but believing offspring with true Christian faith are strong in the Lord. They add more value to our homes than a safe stuffed with money and jewelry. Their eternal souls are treasures in our households now and in our heavenly home forever. One reason Israelite families longed for children was that they knew one of those babies would be the Messiah. Jesus Christ is the ultimate seed who accomplished His mighty deliverance on earth, now reigns in might in heaven, and will return one day to be acknowledged by all as the mightiest of the mighty. Because of His atonement, we and our children who possess saving faith have the righteousness of Christ, which will never fail.

Christ's enduring righteousness is the reason we can hope. He dispels our darkness with His dawning light. In verse 4 the psalmist says, "Unto the upright there ariseth light in the darkness: he is gracious, and full of compassion, and righteous." Christ the Son rises to dispel the black shroud of our deepest and darkest night. Like the dawning light defines objects and brings color to the world, Christ defines all of life and brings joy and meaning to it. Before His face, the powers of darkness flee. In all our dealings with others, we ought to mirror Christ's graciousness, compassion, and righteousness. When we demonstrate His love by ministering as His hands and feet, we incarnate Christ's compassion.

As we read the characteristics of a godly person (v. 5), we see that he or she exhibits kindness, generosity, and discreetness that remind us of the Spirit's fruit (Gal. 5:22–23). Such attributes seem increasingly rare in today's society, even within the church. We are quick to gossip, but slow to lend a hand out of true love for others. We spend thousands on vehicles and homes, but pass the collection plate without dropping in even a quarter. We believe people need to accept us just the way we are, so we make little effort to be tactful in our speech or prudent in our actions.

The person who is internally as well as externally righteous has a secure future: "Surely he shall not be moved for ever: the righteous shall be in everlasting remembrance. He shall not be afraid of evil tidings: his heart is fixed, trusting in the LORD. His heart is established, he shall not be afraid, until he see his desire upon his enemies" (vv. 6–8).

Believers stand firm on a foundation of solid rock, Jesus Christ. They don't disappear into the forgetful oblivion of the past because God Himself remembers them. When our hearts are fixed firmly on God, our pulse remains steady. We need not fear when we hear news reports about frightening events in a foreign country or in our familiar neighborhood. We can trust God to *care* for us and to *take care* of all enemies, because our enemies are His enemies. Someday we will view even that last enemy—death—from a victorious vantage point.

Verse 9 reiterates that the godly person gives generously to the poor and his righteousness endures forever. It also tells us that the believer's horn will be exalted in honor. The biblical image of a horn represents power. In this world, God's people are often weak, oppressed, and humiliated. But the reality beyond this ephemeral sphere is that we are strong, powerful, and honored.

This reality makes the wicked very angry: "The wicked shall see it, and be grieved; he shall gnash with his teeth, and melt away: the desire of the wicked shall perish" (v. 10). Even as the wicked grind their teeth in anger, they dissipate like a morning mist fades under the sun's rays. The desires of their evil hearts and all their schemes and stratagems eventually will disappear.

But we and those of our children who delight in God's Word will remain strong and steadfast. We will rejoice as His light dawns and drives away the darkness of our deepest night.

Questions for Reflection

What is my attitude toward God's authority and His commandments?

How can I incarnate Christ's compassion to others today?

In what ways might I need to be more kind, generous, or discreet?

6

WHOLE HEART

Scripture Reading: Psalm 119:1–8 (Aleph)

*Blessed are they that keep his testimonies, and that seek him
with the whole heart.*
                                          —PSALM 119:2

Psalm 119 is the epitome of acrostic poetry. Each of its
twenty-two stanzas highlights a consecutive letter, and
that letter also begins all eight verses of the section. This
complex construction forms the trellis on which the vine of
heartfelt prayer climbs and blooms with delight in God and
His Word.

The first section of Psalm 119 is named for the first
Hebrew letter, Aleph. This stanza's first three verses are
not part of the prayer that comprises the rest of the psalm.
Speaking in the generic third person, the psalmist begins
with two beatitudes: "Blessed are the undefiled in the way,
who walk in the law of the LORD. Blessed are they that keep
his testimonies, and that seek him with the whole heart.
They also do no iniquity: they walk in his ways" (vv. 1–3).

The person who lives a pure and blameless life is blessed,
but we know that no one is without sin (Rom. 3:10–12) and
even our best works are polluted like a stained garment

(Isa. 64:6). Yet God views believers as clothed in the white linen of Christ's righteousness (Rev. 7:9–13). Being covered with His righteousness doesn't mean we can do whatever we want. These verses show that we need to make an effort to live godly lives, keeping His testimonies and refraining from sin as we walk in God's ways.

Note especially how verse 2 stresses seeking God with the "whole heart." More than merely adhering to external rules, we should wholeheartedly long for an internal relationship with the Lord. Wholeheartedness does not equal religious fervor. Far too many people in our churches are quick to judge or condemn those they perceive as less godly. Like Saul, who later became Paul, they firmly believe they are being zealous for God's truth when they push forward power-driven personal agendas. They disregard or bully people they consider inferior, and view themselves as elite believers.

True piety springs from a humble heart. The meek believer continually digs into the depths of the heart to root out pride, bitterness, and other tenacious sins. To seek God with our whole heart means to love and serve Him devotedly and humbly, allowing the sharp hoe of God's Word to continually cultivate and soften our heart.

This is not a call to the sort of legalism where we quote chapter and verse in support of the law's every letter. It is a directive to allow the law's spirit to shape our spirits. Without this internal motivation, virtuous outward behavior is shallow hypocrisy, a superficial piousness. A wholly devoted heart strives to direct every inward inclination toward genuine humble piety.

When we love God with our whole heart, we live more and more for Him, walking in His ways and keeping His precepts. Is this easy? No—the psalmist begins his prayer to God by acknowledging his inability to keep divine requirements: "Thou hast commanded us to keep thy precepts diligently. O that my ways were directed to keep thy statutes! Then I shall not be ashamed, when I have respect unto all thy commandments" (vv. 4–6).

If the psalmist didn't struggle with keeping God's statutes, he wouldn't confess his failure. This cry shows that he longs to conquer his shortcomings and live as he should, but he knows he can't do this on his own. He needs the Father's direction. Through the Spirit's equipping power, we become capable of fixing our eyes upon Jesus. Those who focus on the triune God and allow the gospel to guide private as well as public behavior will never be ashamed.

A fully devoted heart is upright and teachable: "I will praise thee with uprightness of heart, when I shall have learned thy righteous judgments. I will keep thy statutes: O forsake me not utterly" (vv. 7–8). We should never think we've arrived spiritually. As long as we live, we progress in our sanctification journey through many ups and downs and learn more scriptural truth. In this life, we'll never achieve perfection, and we can't possibly exhaust the Bible's wealth of instruction. But when we pursue truth with teachable spirits and humble hearts, God will guide us. Then we can offer God our wholehearted praise, knowing that He will never forsake us.

How seriously does God view a humble attitude? Because this "whole heart" theme is repeated frequently in Psalm 119, we can be sure it is important. We see just how essential it is in God's sight when we read what He says in other texts.

When David charged his son Solomon to build the temple for the Lord, he urged him to serve God with a whole heart and a willing mind, reminding him that the Lord searches all hearts and understands all imaginations of thought. He warned him not to forsake the Lord lest he be cast off forever (1 Chron. 28:8–10). Serious, indeed!

Even though faithless Israel polluted the land with the idolatry of nature worship, God viewed that blatant spiritual adultery as no worse than Judah's pretense of godly worship. God told Jeremiah that Judah had not turned to Him "with her whole heart, but feignedly" (Jer. 3:9–11). Pretense is as bad as spiritual prostitution!

In a terrifying text, Jesus said He will tell people who did marvelous things in His name, even prophesying and casting out demons, "I never knew you: depart from me" (Matt. 7:21–23). To the hearer of all thoughts, heart attitude speaks louder than hand action.

Many people appropriately use the following text to support calls for national prayer and repentance, but they tend to skim over the first part: "If my people, which are called by my name, shall humble themselves, and pray, and seek my face, and turn from their wicked ways; then will I hear from heaven, and will forgive their sin, and will heal their land" (2 Chron. 7:14). Notice whom God is addressing in this verse. He isn't talking to the godless pagans of our society; He's speaking to the people in the pews, to you and to me.

Let's humble ourselves and turn from our proud ways. Pray that the Spirit will prune our pride so that our love for God blooms as we live for Him with a whole heart!

Questions for Reflection

How has looking at this section of Psalm 119 changed my view of what "whole heart" means?

If I really dig into the hidden depths of my heart, what prideful attitudes need to be rooted out?

What specific actions can I take today, by the Spirit's grace, to demonstrate that I love God with a whole heart?

7

YOUTHFUL ENTHUSIASM

Scripture Reading: Psalm 119:9–16 (Beth)

I will delight myself in thy statutes: I will not forget thy word.
—PSALM 119:16

Who doesn't love to see the excitement of young people? My husband and I enjoy teaching fourth-grade catechism because our students are eager to learn and enthusiastic to share. Some raise their hands so animatedly they almost fall from their chairs!

This section of Psalm 119, structured around the second Hebrew letter, *beth*, reflects a young person with confident faith. Perhaps you have been praying for a young person whose faith is shaky or who is going through major changes or personal struggles. If your burden intensified as you read these verses, I pray that God's Spirit will comfort you and enable you to trust God's sovereignty over this heart-rending grief.

Verse 9 begins by asking how a young person can maintain purity in all avenues of life's walk. The answer is to guard your way according to God's Word. This is simple to say, but difficult to do. Many young people could save themselves and their families a great deal of grief if they would read the Bible as an instruction manual for life. Older folks also benefit from using biblical directives to guide their lives and guard their hearts.

As we saw in the previous meditation, we must seek God wholeheartedly: "With my whole heart have I sought thee: O let me not wander from thy commandments" (v. 10). This recalls the words of a hymn we sometimes sing, "Prone to wander, Lord, I feel it. Prone to leave the God I love." Asahel Nettleton, an American theologian and pastor influential in the Second Great Awakening, wrote "Come, Thou Fount of Every Blessing" in 1825, shortly before he became involved in a controversy with Charles Finney, whose Arminian theology and results-focused methods he opposed. Nettleton took a different approach in his evangelistic efforts, believing that only God's sovereign grace saves sinners rather than embracing Finney's conviction that man's free will, aroused by the evangelist, saves sinners.

Having seen new converts become too attached to evangelists, Nettleton would not stay where people appeared to rely on him. He considered himself only an instrument, leading listeners to focus on personal repentance and God's mercy. He worked alongside faithful local ministers who could maintain long-term relationships with new believers. He also had no use for the misguided zeal then known as "enthusiasm."

That imprudent enthusiasm differs from the eagerness of true faith. Nettleton realized that true Sprit-worked passion arises from a heart devoted to God. Like John Calvin, he offered his heart to the Lord promptly and sincerely. After confessing in his hymn the personal predilection to wander, he concludes: "Here's my heart, O take and seal it; / Seal it for Thy courts above."

All of us, but teens in particular, are prone to wander from the God we previously loved. Some young people stray so far we despair of ever seeing the wayward lamb return to the fold. But as we continue to pray for that precious child, we take comfort in knowing that God has sealed the hearts of His children. In His perfect timing, He will bring His chosen back.

Young people often hurtle along life's path with zealous abandon. But sometimes even older believers do that. We all need the equipping grace of the Holy Spirit to walk in God's ways, and we can't know God's will if we don't study His commands. As we ask the Spirit to keep us on the right path, we must learn God's Word. The psalmist says, "Thy word have I hid in mine heart, that I might not sin against thee" (v. 11).

Although we should continue to commit Bible texts to heart at any age, there's good reason to encourage—even require—children to memorize Scripture. Any adult who attempts memorization realizes that it's not as easy as it was at a younger age. Although children likely don't fully understand all the implications of what they learn, years later they may find themselves in situations when a long-buried text leaps to mind, suddenly becoming meaningful and personal. Why not impart as much biblical instruction as possible while young people are still enthused about learning? Like the psalmist, adults as well as children ought to ask God to instruct them: "Blessed art thou, O LORD: teach me thy statutes" (v. 12). Our Lord is the Master Teacher. He deserves all our praise and honor. Those of all ages who seek

God's direction will confess His truth: "With my lips have I declared all the judgments of thy mouth" (v. 13).

Public Christian witness is difficult for all of us. It's easier to overlook a coworker's comment than use it as an opening for sharing your faith. We all tend to keep our faith to ourselves, especially college students in the hostile environment of secular schools. It's particularly tough for young people to apply their personal faith to their professional choices. They often aim educational efforts toward helping them choose lucrative careers. But what does the psalmist prefer? He says, "I have rejoiced in the way of thy testimonies, as much as in all riches" (v. 14). Career-driven young people—and believers of any age—can find fulfillment and wealth in God's testimonies. Those riches surpass the highest status and most profitable position. But reveling in God's precepts isn't possible without perusal: "I will meditate in thy precepts, and have respect unto thy ways. I will delight myself in thy statutes: I will not forget thy word" (vv. 15–16). The psalmist decides to meditate on and delight in God's Word. He is confident that he will not forget biblical directives.

Focused meditation on Scripture leads to delight in it. By the gracious equipping of God's Holy Spirit, the person—young or old—who remembers biblical teachings will find joy throughout all of life. They will never lose their youthful enthusiasm for Christ.

Questions for Reflection

In what ways should I imitate or avoid youthful enthusiasm?

How can I rely more on God's sovereign care for the way-ward person I love?

What can I do today to express Christ's love enthusiastically to others?

WIDE-EYED SOJOURNER 8

Scripture Reading: Psalm 119:17–24 (Gimel)

Open thou mine eyes, that I may behold wondrous things out of thy law.
—PSALM 119:18

"I am a stranger in the earth," writes the psalmist in the third section of Psalm 119, whose eight verses begin with the Hebrew letter *gimel*. We are all sojourners. This world is not our home. Its trials and tribulations keep us from becoming too complacent and comfortable. We increasingly anticipate the permanent, heavenly dwelling Jesus promised to prepare for us (John 14:2–3).

But while we live on this earth, we don't simply survive the present as we look to the future like a plodding horse wearing blinders. God's grace removes our natural blindness so that we may see His blessing and beauty. "Deal bountifully with thy servant," the psalmist pleads with God, "that I may live, and keep thy word. Open thou mine eyes, that I may behold wondrous things out of thy law" (vv. 17–18). The request for God's bountiful blessing has a dual purpose: life and obedience. God bestows blessing in every breath we take, and His Spirit equips us to godly service. But an abundant life in Christ can be far more than existence and duty. When we open our eyes to seeing wonder in His law, we journey in joy.

How do you view the Bible when you read it? Perhaps you grew up with strict parents who stressed many rules. You may think of God's law as a cold, harsh list of impossible demands. How might your attitude change if you read with wonder?

A child reads fairy tales with a sense of wonder, and adults may marvel at the genius of fantastic novels. But we can read the Bible with far more amazement and joy because John 17:17 assures us that every word of Scripture is true. We can read biblical truth with awe and delight as God reveals His astounding deeds and amazing grace.

After the psalmist asks God to open his eyes to the wonder of His Word, he calls himself a stranger on earth. Peter echoes this terminology when he writes about believers:

> [You] in times past were not a people, but are now the people of God: which had not obtained mercy, but now have obtained mercy. Dearly beloved, I beseech you as strangers and pilgrims, abstain from fleshly lusts, which war against the soul; having your conversation honest among the Gentiles: that, whereas they speak against you as evildoers, they may by your good works, which they shall behold, glorify God in the day of visitation. (1 Peter 2:10–12)

Peter calls God's people strangers and pilgrims. He urges them to live purely and speak honestly so that even those who accuse them may see their good works and glorify God when Christ returns. Peter and the psalmist both identify Christians as sojourners. Young people act as if they will live forever, but the confident psalmist of the previous stanza now recognizes life's transitory nature.

This awareness sharpens the psalmist's longing for the permanence of the Word. His very soul, his essence, is consumed with constant longing—not for an easy life or even his eternal home—but for God's Word.

Like travelers in a foreign country need a guidebook, we sojourners need the Bible to help us understand what we need to know and to show us the way. God's special revelation complements His general revelation. The creation constantly testifies to the existence of an intelligent and supreme God who loves beauty, order, and variety. But Scripture reveals our sin and need for a Savior. It reveals how Christ lived a perfect life and died a perfect death to pay for our sin and provide salvation. And it also reveals how we can journey in thankful and grateful service for God's great gift. As we travel toward our heavenly home, we increasingly long to read every detail of God's guidebook.

Psalm 119:21 reminds us of the importance of a humble heart. God rebukes, even curses, the proud and insolent. Pride indicates a heart that has strayed from God's commandments. The psalmist declares in verse 22 that he has kept the Lord's testimonies and asks God to take away accusation and contempt. This reminds us of the above verse from 1 Peter, which talks about people who wrongfully charge us with doing evil.

This scorn may come from many quarters. When Psalm 119:23 speaks of princes who sit plotting against the believer, we understand that disparagement may come from persons in authority who manipulate behind the scenes. It may be in the political or business realm, but it may also be from leaders within our faith or family communities. We expect persecution from obvious anti-Christian forces, but the most devastating betrayals are from those who are supposed to love us and look out for our welfare. Presidents and prime ministers, pastors and elders, friends and relatives will sometimes fail us. Even—perhaps especially—when family members or church leaders betray us, we sojourners must meditate on Scripture. That is the best place to seek direction: "Thy testimonies also are my delight and my counselors" (v. 24).

Earthly counselors may be helpful and are sometimes necessary, but we need look no further than the book of Job to see their limits. God's testimonies, however, are faithful counselors that never disappoint. They bring delight as well as direction.

The Bible is a guidebook like no other. It's more than mere words on a page. It is living and active, sharper than any two-edged sword (Heb. 4:12). It is the very word of God, which John equates with Christ Himself: "In the beginning was the Word, and the Word was with God, and the Word was God. The same was in the beginning with God" (John 1:1–2). What a wonder! In ways we can't begin to understand, Jesus is the same Word that lives between the worn covers of your Bible. Join this sojourner in asking God to open our eyes to see His wondrous delights.

Questions for Reflection

How does thinking of myself as a sojourner change my priorities?

How can I widen my eyes to see the Bible's beauty and blessing?

In what specific ways can I foster in myself and others wonder for Christ as the living Word?

9

MELTING SOUL

Scripture Reading: Psalm 119:25–32 (Daleth)

My soul melteth for heaviness: strengthen thou me according unto thy word.
—PSALM 119:28

The Psalms employ remarkably vivid language in describing a wide range of human emotions. While mining Psalm 119's rich vein of verses praising God's law, we discover many gems reflecting different emotional facets. What words better capture emotional distress than "my soul melts"?

This section's soul theme initially appears in verse 25, when the psalmist speaks of his soul cleaving or clinging to the dust. The terms "cleaving" and "dust" recall two important events at the dawn of history. Let's consider how God created man. Moses writes, "And the LORD God formed man of the *dust* of the ground, and breathed into his nostrils the breath of life; and man became a living soul" (Gen. 2:7, emphasis added). God created man from dust in what seems to be a two-step process. First, He shaped dirt into a man shape. Second, He breathed the breath of life into him. Dust became a living soul.

The second event is recorded a little later, after God had made a woman from the man's rib and when He established marriage as a divine ordinance: "Therefore shall a man leave his father and his mother, and shall *cleave* unto his wife: and they shall be one flesh" (Gen. 2:24, emphasis added). The verb "cleave" here indicates an intimate union. When the psalmist says his soul cleaves to the dust, it's as if his soul and the dust are becoming one. He is so distressed that his very essence seems about to disintegrate.

Bowed to the ground with his heavy burden and feeling as if his life is slipping away, the psalmist begs God to revive him according to His Word. He acknowledges God not only as the author of life but also as the author of the Word that promises believers existence and blessing.

Although this may be the most devastating struggle of the psalmist's life, it isn't the first time he has experienced trouble. He has called on God in the past: "I have declared my ways, and thou heardest me: teach me thy statutes. Make me to understand the way of thy precepts: so shall I talk of thy wondrous works" (vv. 26–27).

When the psalmist says he has declared his ways, he implies that he conveyed his problems and confessed his sins. When he cried to God, He answered. In humble recognition of his own limitations, the psalmist prays for additional understanding of God's precepts. He doesn't seek more knowledge from a desire for self-improvement or self-aggrandizement, but because he wants to be able to witness to others about God's wondrous works.

Verse 28 shows the psalmist's great anguish and weakness. His entire being is in such intense distress that he feels his soul melting like a sliver of ice in the hot sun. This description sounds like someone who has experienced trauma. Trauma can happen suddenly, like a plane crash, an earthquake, or an attack, or it can occur over an extended time of prolonged physical or sexual abuse. Whatever event or abuse generates trauma, it creates a sense of disintegration. A person experiences intense fear, helplessness, and loss of control; the very core of existence feels threatened. How aptly the image of a melting soul depicts that feeling of disintegration.

The only hope for healing is Christ the Redeemer. He underwent the trauma of the cross to save sinners like us from the penalty for our sin, and He redeems our physical and emotional suffering. We must learn to listen to His voice rather than the voice of the Accuser or the accusers in our minds. Christ forgives all true believers, and only His Spirit can empower our wounded spirits to forgive those who have betrayed or abused us. Jesus speaks to us in love and integrates all aspects of our being in Himself. The Lord restores the melting soul.

The psalmist indicates in our focus verse that his burden is very heavy, but he also conveys hope in his Lord. Recognizing he can't walk in godly ways on his own, he seeks God's strength while confessing the promise and provision of His Word.

He additionally seeks God's help in avoiding lies: "Remove from me the way of lying: and grant me thy law graciously" (v. 29). The way of lying means more than telling a falsehood; it encompasses a wide range of actions that fall under the category of deceitful living including, but not limited to misrepresentation, gossip, manipulation, and ambiguity. Almost without thinking, we try to save face by speaking half-truths rather than the full truth. We need to ask God for His grace, which is the only antidote to the many manifestations of deceit.

This stanza emphasizes the concept of "the way," especially the true way as opposed to the false. As God's Spirit works in our hearts, we more determinedly love truth. The psalmist declares, "I have chosen the way of truth: thy judgments have I laid before me. I have stuck unto thy testimonies: O LORD, put me not to shame" (vv. 30–31).

The Spirit's work in our lives does not absolve us from personal responsibility. We still face many choices. We should choose to walk in pathways of truth, guided by biblical justice. Our holy God judges things perfectly. We must compare things to His perspective rather than viewing them through the self-centered lens of our sin-clouded minds. How often have pastors or elders heard an admonished sinner say, "I believe God wants me to be happy," or, "This can't be wrong because it feels so right."

When we focus on the Lord, we see things increasingly from a godly perspective. Then we're able to walk more and more faithfully. Instead of clinging to the dust, we cling to God's testimonies—all the ways He witnesses to His righteousness, salvation, and the way of truth. The believer who embraces and never releases God's testimonies will not be ashamed.

This authentic Christian will do more than amble along life's path: "I will run the way of thy commandments, when thou shalt enlarge my heart" (v. 32). When the Spirit expands the shriveled heart, the person cowering in the dust stands, walks, then breaks into an all-out run. The melting soul revives and reintegrates with every aspect of being.

Run in the way of God's commandments!

Questions for Reflection

In what ways do I cling to the dust? What trials make my soul melt?

How does the hope of my Redeemer comfort me in these struggles?

What can I say and do today to help myself and others run in the way of truth?

ENLIVENED LIFE

10

Scripture Reading: Psalm 119:33–40 (He)

Turn away mine eyes from beholding vanity; and quicken thou me in thy way.
—PSALM 119:37

The previous section's melting soul, about to disintegrate, rises to run the enlivened life in Psalm 119's fifth stanza. The psalmist continues His impassioned pleading with God in a series of imperative verbs—all beginning with the Hebrew letter *he*—as these verses show how delight in God's law generates full and vibrant living.

The young person narrator we saw earlier has made decisions about his future and is firmly committed to walking in God's way. The remainder of his prayer explores how the believer lives the new life.

The psalmist begins this section with a plea and a promise: "Teach me, O LORD, the way of thy statutes; and I shall keep it unto the end. Give me understanding, and I shall keep thy law; yea, I shall observe it with my whole heart" (vv. 33–34). The plea is enlightenment; the promise is obedience.

The author then asks God to show him the way of His statutes. Similar to legal code with printed regulations known as statutes, God's statutes are His written and recorded rules. Note that the psalmist asks to learn not simply the statutes, but their *way*. He wants to avoid legalism by moving beyond the mere letter of the law to the spirit of it. He vows to keep God's laws in two ways: faithfully to the end of his days and devotedly with his whole heart.

Although the story of a Christian's life on earth comes to an end, the believer's metanarrative never ends. Existence only gets better for the believer. Life on earth is *good*, heaven will be *better*, but the new heavens and earth will be *best*.

An earlier meditation in this devotional emphasized the need to love God in wholehearted humility, but "whole heart" also means loving God with uncompromising devotion. With all life's cares and concerns, it's easy to fall into habits and practices that fracture our focus. An undivided heart doesn't splinter into differing priorities and loyalties, but puts God first. It is utterly and completely devoted to God.

The psalmist promises sincere devotion to the end of his life on earth. But he knows it's impossible for him to keep God's law perfectly or love God wholly. He seeks God's equipping grace to enable him to make what the Heidelberg Catechism calls "a small beginning" of obedience:

> Q. 114: But can those converted to God obey these commandments perfectly?
>
> A.: No. In this life even the holiest *have only a small beginning of this obedience.* Nevertheless, with all seriousness of purpose, they do begin to live according to all, not only some, of God's commandments (emphasis added).

Those who love God's law *do* begin to obey *all* of His commands. The psalmist's promise to keep God's law wholly is based on his plea, begging God to teach him

His statutes and give him understanding. God's equipping grace enables us not only to keep His commands but also to delight in them. The psalmist asks God for that grace, saying, "Make me to go in the path of thy commandments; for therein do I delight" (v. 35).

As a grandmother of a four-year-old, I regularly initiate elementary discussions about behavior. Is "sharing" with little brother by taking the toy away good or bad? What has Mommy said about that? We do good things because we love and want to obey Mommy and Daddy, but most of all to show that we love and want to obey Jesus.

It's not so different for adults, is it? Sin allures and seems attractive, but we won't have joy in our hearts when we wander from God's path. When we unreservedly love God and other people, which is how Jesus summarized all divine commandments (Matt. 22:37–40), our hearts fill with genuine delight.

As we live in loving relationships with God and others, the Spirit guides us in setting proper priorities: "Incline my heart unto thy testimonies, and not to covetousness" (v. 36). Our sinful natures bend toward selfish wealth and personal prestige, but God's grace straightens our hearts so they are upright. We become capable of loving the truths to which God witnesses. Covetousness deadens all we do with selfish desire. We stumble numbly through life. Focusing on God revives our zombie lurch into a vibrant glide.

Let's look at our focus verse. Do you notice anything unusual about it? "Turn away mine eyes from beholding vanity; and quicken thou me in thy way" (v. 37). It is one of the few verses in Psalm 119 that does not mention God's law. That alone should pique our interest, but we pay even closer attention when we realize it contains this stanza's two repeated actions: turn (also in verse 39) and quicken (also in verse 40).

God is the only one who can turn our eyes from vain pursuits. Only His Spirit can enliven us to walk in a godly way. No wonder the psalmist, in verse 38, expresses his reverent and devoted service to the Lord. He also asks God to confirm His promise. This does not condone attempting to test or manipulate God, but indicates that it is proper to seek God's confirmation.

We often experience a feeling of peace as we recall how God has blessed us in the past or as we review the promises of His Word. This internal confirmation, sometimes verified by external events, increases our awe and respect for God's holiness and majesty.

In the last two verses of this stanza, we see themes repeated for emphasis: "Turn away my reproach which I fear: for thy judgments are good. Behold, I have longed after thy precepts: quicken me in thy righteousness" (vv. 39–40). This turning away of reproach, or the removal of shame, is joined with the goodness of divine rules and judgments. The best way to avoid censure or shame is to live according to God's way of abundant life.

The psalmist concludes this section by expressing great longing for a righteous and restored life. Thousands of self-help books promise the fulfilled life, but we need not look beyond the Bible for the ultimate answer. God's Spirit generates godliness in a truly enlivened life.

May God turn your eyes from vain pursuits and focus them on the vibrant life of loving the Lord and others.

Questions for Reflection

How has this section of Psalm 119 changed my perspective of the fulfilled life?

If I'm honest with myself, what areas of my heart need to become more devoted to God?

What particular actions can I take today to show others the delight of a vibrant life in Christ?

11

DELIGHTFUL LIBERTY

Scripture Reading: Psalm 119:41–48 (Waw)

And I will walk at liberty: for I seek thy precepts.
—PSALM 119:45

Americans cherish their liberty. Each Fourth of July, they celebrate independence with picnics, parades, and fireworks displays. But national freedom pales when compared to Christian freedom. Psalm 119 shows how the believer walks in delightful liberty.

The sixth section of this psalm (crafted around the Hebrew letter *waw*) begins with a request for God's promised mercies and salvation: "Let thy mercies come also unto me, O LORD, even thy salvation, according to thy word" (v. 41). Other versions translate mercies as "loving-kindness," "unfailing love," or "steadfast love." This variety in translations begins to convey the comprehensive meaning of the Hebrew word *chesed* (or *hesed*). Simply put, it represents God's covenant love and unfailing faithfulness to His people, who don't deserve it and are often unfaithful.

Salvation in the same sentence directs our attention to God's greatest manifestation of mercy, Christ's atonement.

In his commentary on this passage, John Calvin notes that mercy is mentioned first, and then salvation to put "the cause before the effect" and to show "there is no salvation… but in the pure mercy of God." God's mercy and Christ's atonement set us free from the chains of sin's slavery. We walk unshackled in Christian freedom.

Biblical truths provide the answers we need for every accusation: "So shall I have wherewith to answer him that reproacheth me: for I trust in thy word" (v. 42). Christians often are reproached or taunted. Family members discourage, coworkers disparage, friends betray, enemies persecute, and Satan continually accuses. Nearly all believers battle temptations to doubt their judgment, their work, their actions, even their faith. Victory is possible only by trusting in God's Word. His promises provide all the ammunition we need to silence external and internal taunters.

This trust equips us to triumph over accusations on both fronts, mental and verbal. By God's grace, we respond to negative thoughts quickly and effectively, but also to negative speech boldly and vocally: "And take not the word of truth utterly out of my mouth; for I have hoped in thy judgments" (v. 43). When a friend or coworker says something that dishonors God we feel compelled to speak, yet fear paralyzes our vocal cords. But we can ask God to fill our mouths as well as our minds with His truth. We can speak more clearly and boldly when we hope in the Lord's unfailing promises and trust His righteous judgments.

As we hope and trust, we must make efforts to stay firmly fixed in God's Word: "So shall I keep thy law continually for ever and ever" (v. 44). This sounds a bit presumptuous. After all, no one can perfectly keep the law for even a moment—let alone forever. But we know that the Spirit equips us to small beginnings of obedience now and we'll live in perfection forever.

Our focus verse tells us that seeking God's precepts enables us to walk at liberty. The Bible is full of practical guidelines for walking in the freedom found in Christ. Disobedience erects barriers and stumbling blocks on life's path. Those who strive to obey move forward despite setbacks. They may plod through dark valleys and slip into pitfalls, but even then God is with them. He will lead them out of the valley or pit to walk freely in a wide and wonderful place.

Where will God lead you? Your path may be the crucial influence of a mother raising children. It may be a word fitly spoken before coworkers or mercy expressed to employees. God may even call you to testify before political rulers. The psalmist says, "I will speak of thy testimonies also before kings, and will not be ashamed" (v. 46). Who knows what "kings" God may bring us before to witness of Him? Rulers of this earth are influential and powerful. Appearing before them would cause almost anyone to become anxious. But we need not fear: God promises that His Spirit will give us in that very hour the words we should speak (Matt. 10:17–20; Luke 12:12).

Christ appeared to be shamed before earthly rulers, but the reality was that God orchestrated every event surrounding the death of Jesus for His glory. Because of Christ's victory over death, those called by His name need never be ashamed of the gospel (Rom. 1:16). Even if we are treated shamefully in this world, we know that everything is somehow for our good and God's glory (Rom. 8:28).

While the Holy Spirit equips our hands and mouths to ordinary and extraordinary tasks, He also equips our minds and hearts to deeply love and delight in the Word: "And I will delight myself in thy commandments, which I have loved" (v. 47). Here we clearly see this devotional's theme of delight in loving God's law. Delight is a deep and intense joy. The more we immerse ourselves in God's Word, the more we love it. And the more we love it, the more we love God and want to live for Him. In sheer delight, we reach for the Word and lift our hands in praise: "My hands also will I lift up unto thy commandments, which I have loved; and I will meditate in thy statutes" (v. 48).

Every day we should exalt God's commands and hold them before us. But more than that, we should dive into and immerse ourselves in the written Word. Extended meditation lifts our hands and gaze to our risen and reigning Lord, who paid our ransom and set us free. The Heidelberg Catechism's initial question and the first part of its beloved answer reflect the delight of this freedom:

Q. 1: What is your only comfort in life and death?

A.: That I am not my own, but belong—body and soul, in life and in death—to my faithful Savior Jesus Christ. He has fully paid for all my sins with his precious blood, and has set me free from the tyranny of the devil.

Patriotic fervor may tout the concepts of national freedom and individual liberty, but nothing on earth compares to the incredible freedom of those liberated from the tyranny of the devil. That delightful liberty is true cause for celebration!

Questions for Reflection

What freedoms do I hold dear and which ones should I cherish most?

How should I respond to the accusers in my life?

In what ways can I show others the delight of walking at liberty in Christ?

12

LIVING COMFORT

Scripture Reading: Psalm 119:49–56 (Zayin)

This is my comfort in my affliction: for thy word hath quickened me…. I remember thy judgments of old, O LORD; and have comforted myself.
                                                                —PSALM 119:50, 52

The previous meditation concluded with a focus on our comfort in Christ. This seventh section of Psalm 119 also speaks of comfort that is found in God's Word. We see the link between the two when we consider that Christ is the Word made flesh.

The stanza begins with a rather curious request. The psalmist asks God to remember. Why ask God to remember something when He never forgets anything? "Remember the word unto thy servant, upon which thou hast caused me to hope" (v. 49). Such requests in the Bible are not because God forgets, but because we do. Asking Him to remember His promises reminds *us* of them and rekindles hope when it slumbers within dying embers. God's Spirit fans flickering flames into hope-filled fire.

The Spirit also comforts us in affliction (v. 50). No one lives an adversity-free life. Some people seem to experience more than their fair share of troubles, while others appear to have few difficulties. Although we all know someone who is quick to share every little problem, many people keep their struggles to themselves. We often don't know the extent of their suffering. Some carry secret sorrows that grieve their hearts more than we can imagine. Few who suffer chronic physical pain or mental anguish share it with others. We all have afflictions and we all need comfort.

The psalmist writes that we have comfort because God's Word gives us life. In the Bible, God reveals His plan of salvation and how Christ's atonement grants us eternal life. This life-giving truth is the firm foundation that supports the comfort God provides during the difficult afflictions we face in our earthly sojourn.

Many adversities come from the actions or speech of others, demonstrated in these verses between and after our focus verses: "The proud have had me greatly in derision: yet have I not declined from thy law…. Horror hath taken hold upon me because of the wicked that forsake thy law" (vv. 51, 53).

While the righteous remember God and His promises, the unregenerate forget about God. Ungodly people and institutions wreak havoc upon Christ's church. Wicked rulers and evil people oppress and persecute believers. Governments enact sinful laws and courts render unrighteous judgments. Some decisions make us recoil in horror.

We expect to suffer at the hands of the wicked, but we are appalled when we suffer from the actions or words of those who claim to be Christians. Pride is the most insidious sin within the church. How many times have you sat with a group of believers around a table at a church meeting or fellowship meal listening to someone criticize another Christian? Not all derision is so obvious. Gossip often masquerades under the thin guise of "sharing" concerns. Many church members excel at working behind the scenes to undermine others for "the good" of the church. Some people tell themselves they are acting zealously for Christ's kingdom while they are actually promoting personal empires.

Whether adversity comes from within or outside the church, we can comfort ourselves by remembering God's judgments of old (v. 52). God has never allowed sin to go unpunished. Time after time He worked miraculously for His people. He brought the Israelites out of Egypt (Exodus 1–15). He made Balaam's donkey speak, and He caused the prophet to bless instead of curse (Numbers 22–24). He delivered Jerusalem from Sennacherib (2 Kings 19:32–37; 2 Chron. 32:20–23). Even if we don't see such miraculous deliverances, we know God is sovereign over all that happens to us, and Jesus will return one day to make everything right.

As we pilgrims walk toward our final home, we sing God's righteous songs much as the Jews sang songs of ascent on the way to worship in tabernacle or temple: "Thy statutes have been my songs in the house of my pilgrimage" (v. 54). Our bodies are decrepit tents that will soon wear out, but while we still travel, we can sing God's words back to Him in praise and worship. We can sing His songs as we live and work. We can echo His words as we write or speak what is true and excellent. We can fill our temporary homes with joyful songs that reflect biblical truth.

Repeating the refrain of God's past actions and His present promises comforts us like a mother's gentle lullaby. The psalmist says, "I have remembered thy name, O LORD, in the night, and have kept thy law. This I had, because I kept thy precepts" (vv. 55–56). The Lord is both the almighty sovereign God and our loving heavenly Father. His name alone comforts and upholds us during the anxious or painful hours of seemingly endless insomnia. This blessing comes only to those who love God and keep His commandments.

Keeping God's commandments is its own blessing. We tend to think that God will reward us for keeping His law, but the psalmist shows that obedience itself is the blessing— a blessing that comes from the tender hand of our loving heavenly Father.

We are saved only by God's grace in Jesus Christ through the one-time regenerating work of the Holy Spirit in our hearts. The equipping power of the Spirit increasingly puts the old self to death and brings to life the new. The Heidelberg Catechism explains this "coming-to-life of the new self" in answer 90: "It is wholehearted joy in God through Christ and a delight to do every kind of good as God wants us to." We keep God's precepts because Christians rejoice in doing good and living in God's will. Our joy is not merely a fleeting feeling of happiness, but a deep-rooted delight based on biblical knowledge. From this firm foundation springs a desire to show God, ourselves, and others our gratitude for the great gift of salvation through Jesus Christ.

As we walk through lives riddled with affliction, God Himself comforts us through the fulfilled and future promises of His living Word.

Questions for Reflection

How has God comforted me in the past, and how does that comfort me today?

What sins of pride need to be eradicated from my heart and lips?

In what ways can I sing God's songs of living comfort to others?

13 CHRISTIAN COMMUNITY

Scripture Reading: Psalm 119:57–64 (Heth)

I am a companion of all them that fear thee, and of them that keep thy precepts.
—PSALM 119:63

Do you ever feel that you don't belong? Maybe you lack a close-knit family or a tight group of friends. Maybe everyone at church seems to move in their own circles. But if you believe in Jesus Christ, you're part of a wonderful community. The Spirit assures believers that they are children of God and co-heirs with Christ (Rom. 8:16–17). All Christians are part of this family. And no one can kick you out because no one can snatch you from Christ's hand (John 10:28–29).

The eighth section of Psalm 119 emphasizes our relationship with God and our relationships with other believers. It begins with a confession and a vow: "Thou art my portion, O LORD: I have said that I would keep thy words" (v. 57). What does it mean to call God our "portion"? We think of portion as a part of something bigger, like a house and acreage sold separately from the rest of a farm. Or we may think of losing weight by eating smaller portions. Obviously this verse doesn't portray God as part of anything. Portion here (and in similar texts) refers to our share in God Himself and the divine inheritance He bestows on His children. Through Christ, all believers belong to the same family and share in that inheritance.

Note the order of the phrases in verse 57. God doesn't become our portion because we keep His Word. Rather, because He is our portion, we're able to keep His Word. And His Spirit equips us to publicly confess our determination to do that.

Determination surges through the next three verses as the psalmist prays for mercy while making strong personal commitments: "I intreated thy favour with my whole heart: be merciful unto me according to thy word. I thought on my ways, and turned my feet unto thy testimonies. I made haste, and delayed not to keep thy commandments" (vv. 58–60). The psalmist did four things: he entreated with his whole heart, he considered his own ways, he turned his feet toward godliness, and he obeyed quickly.

The humble and undivided heart seeks God's favor and trusts in His merciful Word. Even if we believe we're serving God with humility and devotion, we are called to examine our motivations and methods. Thinking about what we do and why we do it helps us recognize and repent of sins. Genuine repentance goes beyond feeling sorry for the sin to actually turning from it. The Christian sister who realizes her "concern" is actually gossip stops talking about others. The brother who recognizes his "zeal" as a personal power play stops pushing his own agenda and humbly submits to others.

Verse 60 shows us that we shouldn't be slow or reluctant in examining ourselves or changing behaviors. We must make haste. We can confess our sins in private, but also in safe settings within our faith communities. Fellow believers can help us keep commitments and hold us accountable.

Turning from sin toward God's testimonies doesn't mean we'll be strolling down easy street. Deceitful people will prey on or persecute us. Concerns and pain will keep us up some nights. But God's Word sustains us. The psalmist testifies, "The bands of the wicked have robbed me: but I have not forgotten thy law. At midnight I will rise to give thanks unto thee because of thy righteous judgments" (vv. 61–62).

Remembering the Word guides our reactions when wicked people sin against us. Recalling God's promises renews our hope during lonely watches of the night. Even in times of distress, we are able to lift our spirits in thankful praise. What an example we have in Paul and Silas. Despite bleeding backs and shackled ankles, they sang midnight praise. That prayerful praise was a prelude to God's powerful deliverance as He broke their physical fetters and their jailer's spiritual bonds.

Although there may be times when a Christian is an isolated victim or a lonely sufferer, our focus verse reminds us that believers belong to a huge two-part community. Part of that community is in heaven—the saints who have gone on to glory. But every true believer on earth is part of the current global Christian community.

Brothers and sisters in Christ frequently bless and edify us. We sometimes call Christian fellowship "the communion of saints," a phrase from the Apostles' Creed. This companionship exceeds camaraderie to encompass sharing in Christ and all His benefits. Here's how the Heidelberg Catechism explains it:

Q. 55: What do you understand by "the communion of saints"?

A.: First, that believers one and all, as members of this community, share in Christ and in all his treasures and gifts. Second, that each member should consider it his duty to use his gifts readily and cheerfully for the service and enrichment of the other members.

What an incredible privilege to share in Christ with all His treasures and gifts! It is a privilege, however, that comes with personal responsibility. We are duty bound to use our gifts "readily and cheerfully" (*not* reluctantly or grudgingly) to serve our Christian companions and enrich their lives. We should seek out and develop relationships with committed believers. Then we need to deepen those friendships with mutual encouragement and personal accountability.

God's goodness shines not only in Christian unity but also in creation beauty. The psalmist bursts into praise as he considers how the earth teems with God's mercy: "The earth, O LORD, is full of thy mercy: teach me thy statutes" (v. 64). Overwhelmed with awe at the profusion of divine favor, the psalmist fervently seeks understanding of biblical wisdom. God's mercy pulses through His vivid creation, His vibrant church, and His living Word. We experience it personally in the compassion of the members of our Christian community, our truly forever family.

Questions for Reflection

What does it mean to me that God is my portion?

How can I regularly practice genuine self-examination?

In what new ways can I use my gifts readily and cheerfully to serve and enrich others?

14

AFFLICTION'S TREASURE

Scripture Reading: Psalm 119:65–72 (Teth)

*I delight in thy law. It is good for me that I have been afflicted;
that I might learn thy statutes. The law of thy mouth is better
unto me than thousands of gold and silver.*

—PSALM 119:70–72

Do you treasure affliction? I don't! But this stanza of Psalm
119 shows affliction's value, especially in increasing our
delight in biblical riches.

The psalmist begins this *teth* section by confessing God's
provision and professing his faith: "Thou hast dealt well
with thy servant, O LORD, according unto thy word. Teach
me good judgment and knowledge: for I have believed thy
commandments" (vv. 65, 66). In Hebrew, both verses begin
with "good" as do verses 68, 71, and 72. The psalmist wants
to emphasize God's goodness in all His dealings with His
people. Time after time, the Bible shows God's faithfulness and goodness in caring for His people. An awareness
of God's promises and their fulfillment in the past helps the
psalmist (and us) recognize God's goodness in the present. He believes God's Word but doesn't think he knows
everything. His request for good judgment and knowledge

demonstrates a teachable spirit seeking continued instruction from the Word.

He next admits that affliction has shown him the error of his ways: "Before I was afflicted I went astray: but now have I kept thy word" (v. 67). God used affliction in the psalmist's life to turn him around. As he wandered away from God's Word, the Shepherd's crook pulled him back onto the path of obedience. No matter why or how we are afflicted, difficulties provide opportunities to assess our relationship with God and our obedience to Him. When we recognize a trial as the consequence of our own sin, we need to repent of and reject that sin. If our own sin didn't cause our suffering, we still can see ways to turn more toward God. We know from the biblical account of Job that suffering isn't necessarily the result of a specific sin, but sin in general permeates our broken world and causes all our troubles. God doesn't always use affliction as punishment, but He always uses it as instruction.

As we recognize our sin and return to godliness, we become more aware of God's holiness and righteous actions. "Thou art good, and doest good; teach me thy statutes" (v. 68). This verse links an acknowledgment of God's goodness to a declaration that He does good. All that God does is good, from His creation of light at the finite dawn of recorded history to His banishment of night in the endless day of the eternal city (Rev. 21:22–25). God's character and activity are both good, even in our affliction. Again, the psalmist displays his teachable spirit with a prayer for increased knowledge.

Sadly, affliction frequently springs from the actions and words of other people. This was true for the psalmist, who says, "The proud have forged a lie against me: but I will keep thy precepts with my whole heart. Their heart is as fat as grease; but I delight in thy law" (vv. 69–70). Like a counterfeiter printing fake bills in a windowless basement, the proud person forges lies for personal gain. Many liars are amazingly articulate, wielding pious words that few feel able to refute. Verbal sparring may only increase the damage. The best response could be a silent one, living a godly and quiet witness while trusting God to judge between us and our accusers. When falsely charged, we can join the psalmist in wholeheartedly obeying God's Word.

The heart is composed of cardiac muscle. A healthy heart works smoothly, ceaselessly pumping blood throughout the circulatory system. Fat is the opposite of muscle. Fat takes no action. A lazy, self-indulgent lifestyle expands fat. Do you have the healthy heart of humility or the fat heart of pride?

How do you put your heart on a diet? Try regularly feeding on the nourishing meat of Scripture. The more you eat, the more you develop a taste for it and relish it.

Our obedience supersedes stoic compliance and becomes joyful submission to God's will. Such submission enables us, like the psalmist, to admit that even affliction is good: "It is good for me that I have been afflicted; that I might learn thy statutes" (v. 71). Affliction is good because it drives us to our knees and deeper into God's Word. It strips away our self-confidence and pride. We learn to lean more on the Lord. We dig into the depths of the Bible, discovering its priceless worth and mining its unrivaled riches. "The law of thy mouth is better unto me than thousands of gold and silver" (v. 72).

Imagine rubbing your fingers over a smooth gold coin. Now envision yourself standing before an open chest, mounded so high with treasure that coins are sliding to the ground—thousands of gold disks glinting in the light! You can't comprehend it. Your small pockets can hold only a few pieces of that vast fortune.

God's Word is incomparably richer than all the wealth you can possibly imagine, and affliction can be the prized key that unlocks God's treasure chest. Open the strongbox of God's Word. Treasure overflows. Your pockets are too small, but it's all yours. Pick up the gold and marvel as it dazzles your mind with its illuminating light.

Questions for Reflection

How might God be using my affliction to turn me back to Him?

In what ways might pride be clogging the arteries of my heart?

How does viewing affliction as a prized key change the way I'll live today?

15

DUAL CREATION

Scripture Reading: Psalm 119:73–80 (Yodh)

Thy hands have made me and fashioned me: give me understanding, that I may learn thy commandments.
—PSALM 119:73

God is the Creator of both physical and spiritual life. The tenth stanza of Psalm 119 (patterned according to the Hebrew letter *yodh*) praises the One who fashions people and whose Spirit generates understanding. Our focus verse crystallizes this dual creation.

It reminds me of Elihu's confession: "The spirit of God hath made me, and the breath of the Almighty hath given me life" (Job 33:4). Elihu was one of Job's counselors or comforters, both of which are misnomers for the others, who blamed Job for his problems. But Elihu was different. As the youngest, he waited until the older men had their say and Job had responded. But then he spoke, admonishing all of them and reminding them of God's righteous sovereignty and man's insignificance (Job 32–37). He is like a warm-up speaker, preparing the listeners for the main event when God makes the same points far more forcefully (Job 38–41). Elihu may have been the youngest man sitting around the ash heap with Job, but he was the one who spoke the most truth. And, similarly to this section of Psalm 119, he began his speech by confessing God's creative and regenerative power.

In the first part of Psalm 119:73, the psalmist emphasizes physical creation by praising God for making and fashioning him. The language of making and shaping brings to mind this well-known gem from Paul's letter to the Ephesians: "For we are his workmanship, created in Christ Jesus unto good works, which God hath before ordained that we should walk in them" (Eph. 2:10). God shapes believers as His masterpieces. But we're not meant to hang idly on the wall. We're created in Christ with the purpose of doing good works. From before time began, God ordained righteous actions He wants us to do.

That ties in with the second part of our focus verse. The psalmist expresses his longing for more understanding, not for worldly wisdom in order to be a successful leader or a popular author, but heavenly wisdom for the purpose of learning God's commandments. The psalmist could not have this desire apart from the regenerating work of the Spirit. The Spirit equips him to understand God's commands and walk in them.

We cannot contribute to our spiritual birth any more than we can play a role in our physical birth. But believers can actively serve the Lord and witness to others: "They that fear thee will be glad when they see me; because I have hoped in thy word" (v. 74). Our lives should display hope-filled joy. Our hope isn't in some nebulous religious concept, but in God's vibrant Word. Our joy is in Jesus. These things should be so obvious that people see us and smile. Our

attitude gladdens their hearts and increases hopeful delight
in their own lives.

This reciprocal cycle of hope and joy helps us see God's
hand in affliction: "I know, O LORD, that thy judgments are
right, and that thou in faithfulness hast afflicted me" (v. 75).
When I think of God's faithfulness, I recall His loving care
for me and my family and the many blessings I've seen in
our lives. I usually don't consider afflictions as evidence of
His faithfulness. But God is faithful even—perhaps especially—in trials.

Do you notice how the psalmist confesses that it is
God who has afflicted him? This is a profession of God's
sovereignty. God controls everything that happens to us.
Consider again Job's story. Recall that Satan had to obtain
God's permission prior to afflicting Job (1:6–12; 2:1–7).
Does this mean that God can do wrong? Absolutely not!
Truth-teller Elihu reminds us that God does not do wrong
or pervert justice (34:10, 12). He tells us that God uses afflic-
tion as instruction (36:8–12), delivers the afflicted by their
affliction, and opens their ears through adversity (36:15).

Affliction demonstrates God's faithfulness. He will
never forsake us in our struggles. Sometimes we see how
God used a particular trial for good, but there are often
times when we have no idea how any benefit could possibly
come from our tragedy. Even then, we can pray for comfort,
like the psalmist: "Let, I pray thee, thy merciful kindness be
for my comfort, according to thy word unto thy servant"
(v. 76). God's steadfast love and covenantal kindness comfort His people. Because we are slow to learn and trouble
dulls our minds, God promises over and over in His Word
that He will never leave us and will always love us.

Affliction makes God's promises come alive as we feel His comfort and experience His mercy. We encounter God more personally and dependently in affliction than we do during our good times. When we feel our spirits ebb, God's Spirit revives us: "Let thy tender mercies come unto me, that I may live: for thy law is my delight" (v. 77). How beautifully the psalmist describes God's compassion as His "tender mercies"! God's love revitalizes life and generates joy. He goes beyond simply sustaining us to fill our spirits with delight.

As we've seen repeatedly, many earthly afflictions are caused by proud people: "Let the proud be ashamed; for they dealt perversely with me without a cause: but I will meditate in thy precepts" (v. 78). The arrogant often pervert truth without cause. If you haven't experienced this yet, simply wait. When I receive unjust treatment, I want to protest—loudly and widely. I want everyone to know that I did nothing to instigate this attack. In contrast, the psalmist responds by meditating on God's precepts. Throwing yourself on God's mercy and immersing yourself in His Word is the only antidote to an unjustified assault. We may want to shame the accuser, but that is not our responsibility. We should ask God to take care of it and trust Him to do so.

As we immerse ourselves in biblical truth and trust, we will find companionship among other believers. They will be attracted to our quiet and godly witness, and we will experience the communion of the saints. Those who know God's Word will recognize it being lived in us. "Let those that fear thee turn unto me, and those that have known thy testimonies" (v. 79). We become a strong and united witness of God's love. But personal sin will stain that testimony.

The psalmist requests: "Let my heart be sound in thy statutes; that I be not ashamed" (v. 80). While trusting God to deal with the proud, the humble heart recognizes personal propensity to sin. We need the Spirit's direction to be sound in biblical doctrine and action, lest we bring shame to ourselves and—far worse—to our Lord.

God generates physical and spiritual life. He shapes and fashions us in our mothers' wombs. We are His workmanship, and His Spirit equips us to do His works. He softens and renews our hard hearts. He gives us all we need to live for Him with hopeful joy. Even our afflictions are from His sovereign hand and demonstrate His faithfulness. We can trust God to bring down the proud and build up His church. This God is the Creator who grants life as well as the new life.

Questions for Reflection

What good works did God ordain from before time for me to do today?

How can I show my hope in ways that make other people glad?

In what specific ways can I demonstrate trust in God while responding to my trials?

16

FIERY TRIALS

Scripture Reading: Psalm 119:81–88 (Kaph)

For I am become like a bottle in the smoke; yet do I not forget thy statutes.

—PSALM 119:83

At first glance, this section of Psalm 119 seems depressing. Nearly every verse conveys negative actions and emotions: my soul faints, my eyes fail, the proud dig pits for me, they persecute me, and they have almost consumed me. In a memorable image, the focus verse likens the speaker to a leather bottle or wineskin shriveling in the smoke. But as we get into the two middle stanzas of the psalm, we will see how they reflect a turning point. Woven with the gloomy language of this stanza are God's promises of hope, comfort, and salvation.

The psalmist begins this section by expressing a deep spiritual longing: "My soul fainteth for thy salvation: but I hope in thy word" (v. 81). The psalmist's longing is so intense he feels as if his soul faints. The soul is a person's undying essence. We often feel physically weak or mentally exhausted or emotionally fragile, but at times we may feel a spiritual frailness in our very core. This deep feeling includes both desire and dependence, and it is intrinsically tied to the hope of God's promised salvation.

Would it surprise you to learn that the word "salvation" occurs more times in the Old Testament than in the New? It appears about forty times in the New Testament, but over one hundred times in the Old. More than half of the Old Testament occurrences are in the book of the Psalms, six times in Psalm 119 alone. This psalmist longs for physical deliverance, but he also yearns for spiritual salvation in the promised Messiah.

As the writer's soul hopes for future salvation, he looks for God's comfort during his current distress: "Mine eyes fail for thy word, saying, When wilt thou comfort me?" (v. 82). Feeling as if his spiritual eyesight fails, the psalmist desires to see physical evidence and to feel emotional comfort. Our focus verse shows that he needs God's consolation because his situation is critical. His spirit feels so parched, he describes himself as a shriveled wineskin. Leather repeatedly exposed to smoke shrinks, hardens, and loses its flexibility. It becomes useless. What a fitting picture for the way chronic cares and relentless trials shrivel the spirit!

But the psalmist doesn't dwell on this negative image; he remembers God's statutes. He receives encouragement from reading Scripture and reminding himself of God's faithfulness and fulfilled promises.

In verse 84, the psalmist asks God two very personal questions: "How many are the days of thy servant? when wilt thou execute judgment on them that persecute me?" The chronic character of the psalmist's struggle leads him to question the timing of God's response. It's almost as if he is asking, "How long do I have to put up with this, Lord?" and

"When will these guys get what they deserve?" Don't we often feel like asking these same questions? Trials seem to last forever when we are in the middle of them. When other people mistreat us, we want to see justice done.

We know our personal struggles will end when we die, and we have the assurance Jesus will return one day and make everything right, but God frequently delivers us from struggles while we live. Sometimes we even see His judgment on those who have persecuted us. Deliverance and judgment, however, shouldn't be our goals. Rather we should seek to remain faithful to God's Word and trust His timing during trials.

Did the two questions of verse 84 seem out of character from the rest of Psalm 119? Asking questions is not the only way this verse differs from most in this long psalm. It is one of only a few verses with no specific mention of God's law—an interesting anomaly that attracts attention and piques interest. Perhaps the author's intense pain causes him to depart temporarily from his standard focus on God's law. Possibly the questions create a bond between the psalmist's desire for the promised Savior and our longing for Christ's return. Maybe God wants to assure us that it's all right to ask personal questions—as long as we keep our focus on Him and His Word, which the psalmist returns to in the next verses: "The proud have digged pits for me, which are not after thy law. All thy commandments are faithful: they persecute me wrongfully; help thou me" (vv. 85–86).

The proud person's schemes reflect hatred of God and unwillingness to obey His Word. What a contrast to the faithful psalmist! Time after time he has proclaimed his love for God and delight to do His will. He continues to confess his love for God's law as he protests his innocence and cries to God for help.

God is faithful and His Word is sure, even when we feel life ebb. "They had almost consumed me upon earth; but I forsook not thy precepts. Quicken me after thy lov-ingkindness; so shall I keep the testimony of thy mouth" (vv. 87–88). As the psalmist's strength fades, he desperately clings to God's loving promises. He seeks life, not for his own glory but for God's. He doesn't want to live so that he can enjoy financial success or earthly power. He doesn't even desire leadership in the church or continued fellowship with his family. His singular goal is obedience.

All measures of earthly success are bereft of meaning without biblical obedience. Digging ditches or washing dishes becomes meaningful when performed in obedience to God. Any task can be satisfying when viewed from the perspective of doing God's will in every area of life. But the work of a popular president or respected preacher is mean-ingless if he fails to heed God's law in his private as well as his public life.

Interwoven among this section's negative depictions and descriptions—and the anomaly of questioning God's tim-ing—are the sturdy cords that tie our thoughts to divine faithfulness and comfort and the salvation of the Word made flesh.

When you feel your spirit shriveling in the smoke of your fiery trials, read God's life-giving law and delight in it. Turn your eyes to Christ, the living Word.

Questions for Reflection

In what ways do my deepest desires focus on myself and not on God?

What questions am I asking God?

How can I adjust my goals to honor God and demonstrate my delight in the living Word today?

ENDLESS PERFECTION

17

Scripture Reading: Psalm 119:89–96 (Lamedh)

I have seen an end of all perfection: but thy commandment is exceeding broad.

—PSALM 119:96

The psalmist turns a corner in this stanza of Psalm 119. He climbs from the pit of despair in the previous section by pulling himself up the rungs of the ladder of God's forever faithfulness.

He lifts and fixes his eyes on the blue skies of eternity by contrasting temporal limitations with permanent perfections. This contrast reminds me of the Preacher's oft-repeated theme in Ecclesiastes: "Vanity of vanities…all is vanity…under the sun" (Eccl. 1:2, 3).

Under this earth's sun, our earthly, finite minds and limited vision inhibit our ability to see eternal perfection. We plod through life with the back of our bowed heads feeling the sun's heat, while we gaze at earth's dirt.

In the focus verse, the psalmist tells God how he has witnessed the limits of all earthly perfection and how much God's Word expands the boundaries of our earthly experience. Although all is vanity when considered only in the light of a dying sun, meaning materializes when life is viewed in the radiance of the living Son.

Christ the living Word sits at the powerful right hand of God. All of God's words—from creation to consummation and beyond—remain forever: "Forever, O LORD, thy word is settled in heaven" (v. 89). Heaven is the headquarters for God's Word. Heaven is also the seat of God's unfailing faithfulness: "Thy faithfulness is unto all generations: thou hast established the earth, and it abideth. They continue this day according to thine ordinances: for all are thy servants" (vv. 90–91).

By this time, you might notice something unusual about that first verse. It doesn't fit Psalm 119's usual pattern of specifically mentioning God's law, does it? But the Word is the subtext beneath God's love for His people and His care for their world.

As babies are born and grandparents die, God's faithfulness extends to each succeeding generation of His covenant people. The heavens and earth sprang into being by the power of God's spoken word. According to His command, the world whirls on its axis and planets spin in their places. And our solar system is only a fraction of God's vast universe. He ordained heavens, earth, and all things to exist in service to Him.

But the cosmos will not last forever. Jesus said, "Heaven and earth shall pass away, but my words shall not pass away" (Matt. 24:35; Mark 13:31; Luke 21:33). Christ will renew creation at His return, but God's Word needs no renewal. It is eternal.

That unchanging Word is our only hope when waves of tribulation crash against us and threaten to drown us in the sea of despair. The psalmist testifies, "Unless thy law had been my delights, I should then have perished in mine affliction. I will never forget thy precepts: for with them thou hast quickened me" (vv. 92–93). When affliction strikes, the psalmist finds life and strength in God's written and living Word. He doesn't wait until he is in trouble to read the Bible. It has been his daily study and constant companion. If he didn't have this repository of Scripture in his mind, he wouldn't survive trials. In the Bible and in Christ, we discover multiple delights: hope, joy, comfort, consolation, encouragement, refreshment, and revival.

When enemies attack, the psalmist begs for help on the basis of his standing as God's beloved child. But he doesn't sit back and twiddle his thumbs as he waits for God to act. He continues to study biblical directives: "I am thine, save me: for I have sought thy precepts. The wicked have waited for me to destroy me: but I will consider thy testimonies" (vv. 94–95). God's promises uphold the believer when victimized by those within or outside the church. His Word is our only hope not only in personal struggles but also in public persecution. Rather than seeking revenge, the psalmist seeks God's Word. Christ is the only hope for the victim.

Our focus verse concludes this section by contrasting the limits of perfection to the expanse of God's commandment. Life has its good times and pleasant seasons, but they never seem to last. "All good things must end" we think when a particularly enjoyable phase of life is completed or we face going back to work after a relaxing vacation. The adage reflects the reality of life in a fallen world where good times are only temporary.

People, possessions, and positions disappoint. We will never find perfection in a spouse, child, or parent. No career or status will ever satisfy. If you spend thousands—even millions—building your dream home, you will soon find a hairline crack in a white ceiling or a crawling insect on the basement floor. Nothing under the sun is perfect.

We will never experience earthly perfection, but God is strengthening our faith and sanctifying us in our struggles and will one day make us perfect. Peter wrote, "But the God of all grace, who hath called us unto his eternal glory by Christ Jesus, after that ye have suffered a while, make you perfect, stablish, strengthen, settle you. To him be glory and dominion for ever and ever. Amen" (1 Peter 5:10–11).

This transient existence under the sun will fade in the permanent glory of the Son. In the living Word who became flesh we discover boundless perfection. His Spirit lives with us and dwells in us, gradually perfecting us until the final day when we will begin an eternity of dwelling with Christ in unimaginable splendor.

We anticipate the return of the living Word with hope. And we open God's limitless Word with joy. We look forward to forever with delight.

Questions for Reflection

In what ways can I prepare my mind for the world's inevitable affliction or persecution?

Where do I seek perfection?

What can I do today to demonstrate my trust in Christ and His perfection?

18

SWEET DELIGHT

Scripture Reading: Psalm 119:97–104 (Mem)

How sweet are thy words unto my taste! yea, sweeter than honey to my mouth!

—PSALM 119:103

What does the phrase "sweet delight" bring to mind? Perhaps spending time with a precious person—like a cherished grandbaby or a dear spouse or a favorite friend. Maybe you think of a sweet treat or decadent dessert. But if you've just read the focus verse, you may be thinking of reading the Bible. Imagine all your favorite emotions and pleasures rolled into one delightful experience—when you read God's Word and grow closer to Jesus.

This stanza's sensory language imprints images in our minds and whets our appetite for the Word. Reading the focus verse almost makes my mouth water, while longing and love for God well within my heart. That feeling flows from the familiar first verse of Psalm 119's *mem* section: "O how love I thy law! it is my meditation all the day" (v. 97). Can any of us honestly say God's law is our meditation all the day? Even if you lived as a hermit in a wilderness cave and spent every waking hour reading a scroll of Scripture, would you be able to constantly meditate on it? My mind would soon drift to thoughts of my oldest and dearest friends: me, myself, and I.

The psalmist is not a scriptural superhero. He's human, like you and me, but he loves reading and meditating on the Word. As he goes about his daily tasks, the words he has read reverberate in his mind and initiate communion with God.

That well-known verse 97 is followed by one far less familiar, but which also emphasizes constant communion with God through His commandments: "Thou through thy commandments hast made me wiser than mine enemies: for they are ever with me" (v. 98). This verse reveals a theme we've seen with increasing frequency—the existence of enemies. Why are we surprised when we suffer from the speech or actions of others or when we reel under the onslaught of spiritual warfare? The Bible repeatedly shows us that conflict is an unavoidable part of life. Our fallen world is full of evil. But the psalm's references to enemies are always linked to the victory of biblical wisdom. Through His commandments, God makes us wiser than the craftiest adversary.

The psalmist goes on to assure us that scriptural meditation generates wisdom surpassing that of an intelligent teacher or ancient sage. "I have more understanding than all my teachers: for thy testimonies are my meditation. I understand more than the ancients, because I keep thy precepts" (vv. 99–100). Certainly we can—and should—learn from highly educated and insightful theologians and search the wisdom of teachers through the ages, no matter how lofty our education or how high our IQ; however, we should never believe we have exclusive or superior spiritual knowledge.

That kind of thinking only demonstrates a complete lack of the humility necessary for true biblical wisdom.

But the above verses confirm that any lowly believer can—and should—meditate daily on the Word and trust God to reveal His truth. We know that the "fear of the LORD is the beginning of wisdom" (Ps. 111:10; Prov. 1:7 and 9:10 are similar). Any believer who loves and reveres God begins a lifetime pursuit of true knowledge that even the brightest unbeliever will never know.

The psalmist does more than merely meditate on God's law; he obeys it: "I have refrained my feet from every evil way, that I might keep thy word. I have not departed from thy judgments: for thou has taught me" (vv. 101–2). Notice how mental acquiescence requires physical effort? The psalmist has made a conscious decision to obey and follows that up with bodily refraining his feet from every evil path. He knows what is right because God has taught him, but he also does what is right by not departing from God's judgments.

This call to committed action is followed by our focus verse's familiar morsel, describing God's Word as a sweet delight. I love this image of licking up God's law like golden honey. You may recall how Psalm 19 also described God's Word as sweeter than honey. These biblical directives to crave the Word as intensely as the sweetest treat remind me of David's beautiful imperative in Psalm 34: "O taste and see that the LORD is good: blessed is the man that trusteth in him!" (Ps. 34:8).

Scripture isn't dry toast. It is like roast beef and mashed potatoes or filet mignon with sautéed mushrooms. It is like grilled chicken with wild rice or lobster with butter sauce. It's a veritable feast of delectable delights. We're to desire

God's Word even more than we crave our favorite foods. This stanza concludes with a reiteration that true wisdom comes from knowing God's Word: "Through thy precepts I get understanding: therefore I hate every false way" (v. 104).

We need to devour God's Word and allow it to feed our entire being. Our biblical knowledge shouldn't remain rattling around uselessly in our heads. It should generate mental, emotional, and physical righteousness, which manifest themselves in loving God's law and hating every evil action. Are you hungry? Eat the Word!

Questions for Reflection

What is my sweetest delight?

In what ways am I wiser than even intelligent teachers and ancient sages?

How can I more avidly devour God's Word?

19

ILLUMINATING LAMP

Scripture Reading: Psalm 119:105–112 (Nun)

Thy word is a lamp unto my feet, and a light unto my path.
—PSALM 119:105

Verse 105 could possibly be the most famous of all Psalm 119's 176 verses. It depicts an enlightening theme in a vivid image that shines in our minds. As we learn to delight in God's law, He gives us this visual aid to help us understand how His Word guides us. When we envision God's Word as a lamp shedding light on our every step, nebulous knowledge becomes concrete comprehension.

This section of the psalm describes life as a path along which we walk while we hold before us the radiant lamp of God's Word. His law is the lantern that illuminates our walk through this dark world. We hang on to that light and hold it aloft to show us the firm ground and help us avoid pitfalls. If we can't see the path, we will wander from it. We might fall into a ditch or sink into a swamp. Even if we stay on course, we need to see the fallen branches that might trip us. The radiance of God's law exposes all evil.

We walk life's path with intention and purpose. Walking is an action. We lift our feet and put them down in front of each other. Rather than wander aimlessly, we must stride forward, choosing our direction and moving toward our destination. The psalmist has chosen to keep following the right path: "I have sworn, and I will perform it, that I will keep thy righteous judgments" (v. 106). Do you see the commitment conveyed in those words? He has vowed to obey, and he is determined to do it.

It's easy to think about being more godly, but it takes strong resolve to carry out such a commitment. It's difficult enough when things are going well and life is easy, but it's a lot tougher when life is hard. Let's look at the psalmist's situation: "I am afflicted very much: quicken me, O LORD, according unto thy word" (v. 107). Life isn't exactly easy for him, is it? He's suffering so intensely that he speaks superlatively: "*very* much." His severe affliction causes him to feel his life fade. In this deep distress, he remembers God's assurances and begs Him to revive him in keeping with those promises. We can do the same thing. When we feel life's energy drain away, we can find refreshment in Scripture and ask God for revival.

While the psalmist prays, he also praises: "Accept, I beseech thee, the freewill offerings of my mouth, O LORD, and teach me thy judgments" (v. 108). As he feels life ebb away, he freely offers praise to God and shows his teachable spirit. He willingly submits to continued instruction from the Lord. Like the psalmist, we can do more than pray during times of trial. We can praise and persevere.

We may not find immediate relief. We may continue to struggle, as the writer of this psalm plainly does: "My soul is continually in my hand: yet do I not forget thy law" (v. 109). He feels as if he holds life by the fingertips and his grip is about to slip. Despite this tenuous hold, he still remembers God's law. And in spite of traps and temptations along the way, he does not stray from the straight path of God's commands.

In verse 110 we see again the enemies of God's people: "The wicked have laid a snare for me: yet I erred not from thy precepts" (v. 110). Even when we are not suffering obvious persecution, the devil never relents in attacking Christians. We also constantly suffer the effects of sin in our world and in our own bodies. Yet we must not use problems or suffering as an excuse to sin; rather, trouble should prompt us to be all the more diligent in our obedience. Whatever trials or temptations threaten to trip us, we should not wander from God's way.

The precious lantern of God's law has revealed the enemy's snare to the psalmist. He sees the trap and avoids being caught. He also sticks to the path. Exposing evil is only one of the reasons why he delights in the light. Read how he prizes the Word: "Thy testimonies have I taken as an heritage for ever: for they are the rejoicing of my heart" (v. 111). The psalmist reaches out and grasps hold of Scripture as his eternal heritage. Do you think of God's law as an everlasting inheritance? Do you view it as the joy of your heart? I have to admit I often fail to think of the Bible in these terms. But revering the Word as a priceless heirloom of the faith will help us experience heartfelt joy.

As we see time and again in the psalms, joy flows from obedience. The psalmist says, "I have inclined mine heart to perform thy statutes alway, even unto the end" (v. 112). The joyful heart longs to do God's will, and doing His will generates joy. It's a beautiful cycle of joy in life's journey. As we travel the straight and narrow path, let's join the psalmist in determining to keep God's commands until the very end of our days. Let's resolve to be faithfully obedient until God calls us home.

In this broken world, we often feel as if we're stumbling around in the shadows, don't we? Are you staggering through a dark valley? Does it seem that traps are about to spring on you from every side? Do you feel as if your grip on life has nearly slipped?

Hold on to God's Word. Lift that lamp before you and let it illumine your way. Keep walking forward on the right path. Delight in the light!

Questions for Reflection

What does the image of God's Word as a lamp mean to me?

How can I pray, praise, and persevere in my present struggles?

In what specific ways can I show my joy in God's Word to Him and others today?

20

HIDING PLACE

Scripture Reading: Psalm 119:113–120 (Samekh)

Thou art my hiding place and my shield: I hope in thy word.
—PSALM 119:114

In her book *The Hiding Place*, Corrie ten Boom wrote about the power of God's love over great evil. A Christian who sheltered Jews during the Nazi occupation of the Netherlands, Corrie was arrested and eventually incarcerated in the notorious Ravensbruck concentration camp. *The Hiding Place* was not only a secret room in the Ten Boom home in Haarlem but also the refuge Corrie found in God while experiencing concentration camp horrors. A scene from her childhood quotes her father reading Psalm 119:114, showing how the book's title moves beyond the Ten Booms' hidden room to God as our ultimate hiding place.

Like Corrie and the psalmist, we can find hope in God's Word and a safe haven in His care. Verses 113 to 120 focus on God's sovereignty by contrasting His protection of the righteous with His judgment of the wicked.

The psalmist begins this section with a personal confession that is a contrast: "I hate vain thoughts: but thy law do I love" (v. 113). What are vain thoughts? They might be musings that are arrogant or worthless. I hate the vain thoughts of others, but I cling to my own. I sometimes think too much *of* myself, and I always think too much *about* myself. When I consider the sheer volume of time I spend thinking about myself, my family, my work, and my concerns compared to the fraction spent dwelling on God and His Word, I am ashamed. Do you, like me, waste time and mental energy in arrogant or worthless thoughts? We must learn to recognize those thinking patterns and then work to banish them.

Other Bible versions translate "vain thoughts" as "the double-minded." James describes the double-minded person as a doubter who fails to ask in faith for God's gifts. Such a person is as unstable as a wave driven by the wind (James 1:6–8). Later James urges the double-minded to purify their hearts by rejecting self-centered motives and humbling themselves before the Lord (James 4:3–10). It's easy to point the finger at other people who seem double-minded, but verse 113 encourages us to cultivate humility in our own minds and hearts by redirecting our passions and pursuits from self toward God and His Word.

Our focus verse assures us that God is our sanctuary and our shield. He is a place of refuge as well as our protection in battle. He shelters us, but also calls us to keep fighting rather than withdraw from the fray. We press on with confidence because we have the hope that God's Word kindles in our hearts.

Yet we often become weary. We long to be relieved from the front offensive so we can rest behind lines in the bunker. We wish the enemy would retreat. "Depart from me, ye evildoers," says the psalmist, "for I will keep the commandments of my God (v. 115). This desire for peace has a purpose: obedience. Although turmoil provides unique opportunities to submit and obey, it also saps our energies and narrows our focus. We may exist in survival mode. Peace generates motivation and creativity to look beyond ourselves. We discover new ways to obey God and pour ourselves into His service.

Did you notice anything strange about verse 115? Who is the psalmist speaking to? Evildoers. This is the only verse in the entire psalm, aside from its initial three, that does not directly address God. It's almost as if the psalmist glances up from his prayer and shakes his fist at approaching enemies before again folding his hands. Despite the distraction of attack, he is determined to continue communing with his Lord.

The psalmist reiterates that whatever our circumstances, we hope in God's Word. We need not be ashamed of our faith because God will sustain us: "Uphold me according unto thy word, that I may live: and let me not be ashamed of my hope. Hold thou me up, and I shall be safe: and I will have respect unto thy statutes continually" (vv. 116–17). Even if believers aren't delivered from every attack in this life, God is with them now and will keep them safe eternally. Our response should be continual obedience. If we've been delivered by grace alone through Christ and not because we have earned it, why must we still do good? The Heidelberg Catechism answers this very question in answer 86:

> To be sure, Christ has redeemed us by his blood. But we do good because, Christ by his Spirit is also renewing us to be like himself, so that in all our living we may show that we are thankful to God for all he has done for us, and so that he may be praised through us. And we do good so that

we may be assured of our faith by its fruits, and so that by our godly living our neighbors may be won over to Christ.

Obedience springs from a Spirit-generated desire to be more Christlike as well as to thank and praise God in great gratitude. It also strengthens our assurance and witnesses to others. Doing good is the visible fruit of a tree grafted into Christ (Romans 11).

Although the wicked may appear to triumph over the righteous in this life, God will not allow them to genuinely succeed: "Thou hast trodden down all them that err from thy statutes: for their deceit is falsehood. Thou puttest away all the wicked of the earth like dross: therefore I love thy testimonies" (vv. 118–19). God will trample the disobedient and deceitful. Liars have no place in His kingdom. Believers frequently are purified like fine gold in affliction's flames, but the wicked cannot survive God's refining fire. They are dull dross, which He discards like scum skimmed from the surface of molten metal. We all do well to tremble like the psalmist: "My flesh trembleth for fear of thee; and I am afraid of thy judgments" (v. 120).

We need not fear those who can kill the body, but only the One who can destroy the soul (Matt. 10:28). But fearing God is not quaking in terror. Rather, it's trembling in awe and reverence before His majestic holiness. If Christ has redeemed you, your eternal future is secure. God Himself is your hiding place.

Questions for Reflection

In what ways am I double-minded?

Where do I put my hope?

What can I do today to demonstrate my gratitude to God and witness to others of His great love?

21

SEEING SALVATION

Scripture Reading: Psalm 119:121–128 (Ayin)

Mine eyes fail for thy salvation, and for the word of thy righteousness.
—PSALM 119:123

In this stanza, the psalmist's eyes fail with longing. What he desires to see is God's present and future salvation.

Initially, the writer confesses that he has done what is just and right: "I have done judgment and justice: leave me not to mine oppressors. Be surety for thy servant for good: let not the proud oppress me" (vv. 121–122). Each of these first two verses ends with the psalmist begging God to prevent proud people from oppressing him. He asks God to be his "surety" for good. To be surety is to take responsibility for someone else's performance of an obligation, such as appearing in court or paying a debt. Doesn't this language remind you of our justification? Christ paid our debt of punishment for sin, and God declares us "not guilty" because Christ stood before His tribunal in our place.

In our focus verse, the psalmist seems to anticipate present deliverance from worldly oppressors as well as eternal salvation through the long-awaited and promised Messiah. Jesus Christ is the looked-for living Word of righteousness.

The writer's longing eyes remind me of Job's confession regarding a living Redeemer, who would stand upon the earth one day. Job believed his resurrected body would appear before Him, and with his own eyes, he would see God (Job 19:25–27). Like Job and the psalmist, we so long for final deliverance that our hearts faint and our eyes fail.

Christ's return and judgment will terrify unbelievers, but believers can find comfort in the thought. The Heidelberg Catechism explains why:

> *Q. 52: How does Christ's return "to judge the living and the dead" comfort you?*
>
> A.: In all my distress and persecution I turn my eyes to the heavens and confidently await as judge the very One who has already stood trial in my place before God and so has removed the whole curse from me. All his enemies and mine he will condemn to everlasting punishment: but me and all his chosen ones he will take along with him into the joy and the glory of heaven.

When we are distressed, we can look to Christ and wait for His judgment with confident joy. He already stood trial for us and replaced our guilt with His righteousness. His enemies are our enemies, and they will be condemned. But He will take us into His joy and glory. Comfort indeed!

As we anticipate that great day, we live by God's mercy and Word: "Deal with thy servant according unto thy mercy, and teach me thy statutes" (v. 124). Recognizing his dependence upon God, the psalmist seeks His mercy and the Spirit's equipping power to learn the Word. How does

God deal with His people? Within the context of a covenant relationship, He extends His loving-kindness. As our loving heavenly Father, He teaches us all we need to know to live with joy and die without fear.

Biblical wisdom begins with an awe-filled reverence for God. So the psalmist humbles himself before the Lord, asking for the ability to comprehend His Word: "I am thy servant; give me understanding, that I may know thy testimonies" (v. 125). As a willing servant, the psalmist seeks understanding not for his own advancement but for God's. He wants to increasingly understand God's directives so he can better serve Him. But his eagerness isn't only for personal service. He also is eager for divine action—so keen that his tone sounds almost demanding: "It is time for thee, O LORD, to work: for they have made void thy law" (v. 126). The psalmist is eager for God to uphold His law. When we are impatient for God to act, we need to examine our hearts. Do we want action because we have been hurt? Do we want to get even? We must look past our battle wounds to focus on the uplifted banner of God's Word. While Old Testament Israel looked to the promised Messiah, there were times in its history when disregard for God's Word intensified His people's yearning for the One who would fulfill the law. Perhaps verse 126 expresses an element of that longing.

The psalmist exhibits a Christlike love for God's commandments when he tells God how he values them more than fine gold in verse 127: "Therefore I love thy commandments above gold; yea, above fine gold." Because God saves His people now and for eternity, loves them and teaches them His law, gives understanding to the humble, and will never allow His Word to be broken, the psalmist prizes His precepts as righteous and hates every false path: "*Therefore* I esteem all thy precepts concerning all things to be right; and I hate every false way" (v. 128, emphasis added). This section of the psalmist's prayer has circled from confessing his behavior is right to professing that all God's precepts are right. Because he recognizes God's righteous rules, he realizes he must hate what God hates. Rather than merely seeking to avoid temptation, he asks for a heart transplant so that sin becomes abhorrent and no longer tempts him.

May God act now wherever His law has been broken. May we hate every false path as we see His salvation today and look with comfort to our future with Christ.

Questions for Reflection

When I think about Christ's return and His coming judgment, how do I feel?

What or whom do I serve?

How can I move beyond resisting temptation today to hating what is false?

22

TEAR RIVERS

Scripture Reading: Psalm 119:129–136 (Pe)

Rivers of tears run down mine eyes, because they keep not thy law.
—PSALM 119:136

Do you and I love God's law so much that we are moved to tears when we see people failing to keep it? The previous section showed the psalmist pleading—practically demanding—that God act because His law had been broken. This stanza shows how his love and delight in the Word leads to rivers of tears when he sees it ignored.

These verses begin by extolling God's Word as wonderful: "Thy testimonies are wonderful: therefore doth my soul keep them" (v. 129). For the psalmist, keeping God's commandments isn't a matter of mere emotion (heart) or sterile doctrine (mind). It is a comprehensive obedience that permeates the seat of spirituality and the most integral aspect of being: the soul.

"Wonderful" literally means to inspire wonder. When is the last time you marveled at the Bible's amazing beauty? This study has opened my eyes to the artistic intricacies of Psalm 119's construction as well as the priceless treasure of its content. If we marvel at God's law, our core essence delights in keeping it.

We cannot wonder at the Word if we don't enter and engage the text: "The entrance of thy words giveth light: it giveth understanding unto the simple" (v. 130). Rather than let the Bible sit on a shelf collecting dust, we need to pick it up and open it. But even if we have a habit of reading Scripture daily, routines and traditions become cursory unless we read with an engaged mind and seek meaning through the Spirit's guidance. God's words enter our brains when we unfold the text and unpack its meaning. We don't need an elite organization or a superior person to read the Bible and spoon-feed us its meaning. Reformed Christians confess the clarity (or perspicuity) of Scripture and believe that ordinary people can read and understand the Bible. Even for simple minds, the light of truth shines from between its open covers.

Don't those first two verses of this stanza make you long for God's Word? The psalmist's intense longing is so palpable that in verse 131 he compares it to gasping for air: "I opened my mouth, and panted: for I longed for thy commandments." What an expression of desire! Do I long for God's commandments so intensely that yearning steals my breath away?

The next four verses contain a progression of petitions:

Look thou upon me, and be merciful unto me, as thou usest to do unto those that love thy name. Order my steps in thy word: and let not any iniquity have dominion over me. Deliver me from the oppression of man: so will I keep thy precepts. Make thy face to shine upon thy servant; and teach me thy statutes. (vv. 132–35)

The first and last verses begin with requests for God to look upon the psalmist with favor. In between, we see pleas that remind us of God's faithfulness to those who love Him, His Spirit's equipping power, and the Lord's deliverance from oppression.

Commentators disagree on whether, in the Hebrew, verse 132 is one of the few that doesn't mention God's law. What is clear, however, is that it speaks of God's loving mercy and bases its plea for favor on the undeniable existence of God's covenant relationship with His people.

On that basis, the psalmist asks God to keep his steps steady as he walks in the world according to the directives and promises of the Word. He also prays that God will keep sin from dominating him. Redeemed Christians still sin, but sin no longer controls them. Christ has broken the power of sin and guides us by His Spirit.

After confessing God's relationship with him and his own inclination toward sin, the psalmist begs for deliverance from oppression. He seeks relief so that he can have more freedom to keep God's precepts.

The first part of verse 131 ("Look thou upon me, and be merciful unto me") and especially verse 135 ("Make thy face to shine upon thy servant") reflect the familiar Aaronic blessing from Numbers 6: "The LORD bless thee, and keep thee: the LORD make his face shine upon thee, and be gracious unto thee: the LORD lift up his countenance upon thee, and give thee peace" (vv. 24–26).

The author of Psalm 119 condenses the all-inclusive content of this threefold blessing into the first phrase of verse 135. He then couples that with the second phrase's request for instruction. The fullness of God's shining face lights our lives with blessing and increases our desire to learn His Word and delight in it.

This primarily positive section concludes with a negative image as visual and personal as the open mouth of verse 131. But in our focus verse, our attention shifts from the psalmist's panting mouth to his crying eyes. He isn't merely shedding a tear. No, water gushes from his eyes and runs down his cheeks like rivers. Why does he weep? Because people do not keep God's law.

We live in a broken world in which people suffer or cause others pain. If the whole creation groans (Rom. 8:22), shouldn't we cry? Do our hearts break over our own sin as well as the sin of others?

May we marvel at God's Word, loving Him and it with all our hearts, minds, and souls. May we enter into His Word and His presence with confidence that He welcomes simple sinners. May we delight in His breathtaking Word and weep when we see it broken. May God shine the gracious light of His face upon us and grant us peace.

Questions for Reflection

Do I view Scripture with a sense of wonder?

How can I engage more with the text as I read the Bible?

How can I help those who suffer today because others have broken God's Word?

DIVINE RIGHTEOUSNESS **23**

Scripture Reading: Psalm 119:137–144 (Tsadhe)

Thy righteousness is an everlasting righteousness, and thy law is the truth. Trouble and anguish have taken hold on me: yet thy commandments are my delights.

—PSALM 119:142–143

Praises of the Lord's righteousness ring in the first verse and echo throughout the *tsadhe* stanza. This praise springs from a heart that is both humble and passionate. In spite of attack and anguish, the psalmist prizes and delights in God's Word.

Notice the words reflecting divine righteousness in the first two verses: "Righteous art thou, O LORD, and upright are thy judgments. Thy testimonies that thou hast commanded are righteous and very faithful" (vv. 137–138). Addressing the Lord, the psalmist acknowledges that God is righteous and His Word is upright. From creation to the end of time, God commands, and His righteous decrees come to be. God's Word is trustworthy, and He is faithful, even when we are not. As the living Word, Christ faithfully performed all things necessary for our salvation.

In the previous section, we saw the psalmist shed copious tears over God's broken law. Now we see how his enemies' disregard for God's words causes him to feel consumed by his zeal: "My zeal hath consumed me, because mine enemies have forgotten thy words" (v. 139). Religious zeal sounds negative to our culture-adapted ears. But fervent devotion can be positive, particularly when it is a response to our foes' disregard for God's Word.

This verse brings to mind the accounts of Jesus cleansing the temple (Matt. 21:12–13; Mark 11:15–19; John 2:13–17). According to John, when the disciples witnessed Christ's decisive action, they immediately recalled a similar scriptural phrase about consuming zeal (Ps. 69:9).

Righteous zeal doesn't mean we must preach on street corners or harangue our coworkers, confronting them with their sin. We are not called to be obnoxious, legalistic, or hypocritical. We are called to be passionate in expressing Christ's love. Jesus drove out money-loving merchants who desecrated the temple and He criticized hypocritical leaders, but He also befriended sinners, gently speaking the truth to them in love. God's children should imitate Jesus. We gain perspective on appropriate righteous zeal when we realize that, as the perfect Son of God, Christ Himself became our righteousness and sanctification (1 Cor. 1:30).

In the next verse, the writer proclaims his love for Scripture's purity: "Thy word is very pure: therefore thy servant loveth it" (v. 140). God's Word is more pure than refined gold. Time after time, His promises have been tested and proved true. Reflect on how you've seen them fulfilled in your life. Hasn't He exceeded your needs? Hasn't His Spirit upheld you during overwhelming grief, pain, anxiety, or depression? God has blessed us beyond our imagination and sustained us beyond our endurance. Shouldn't our hearts pulse with love?

Considering God's promises and providence helps us glimpse His majestic perfection and helps us recognize our lowly state. The psalmist confesses, "I am small and despised: yet do not I forget thy precepts" (v. 141). The psalmist realizes his insignificance, especially compared to God and His pure Word. His awareness of God's majesty and his own lowliness shows insight. True wisdom, John Calvin explained at the beginning of his *Institutes of the Christian Religion*, "consists almost entirely of two parts: the knowledge of God and of ourselves."

The psalmist's awareness of the differences between God and himself leads to his close relationship with the Lord, but his other relationships are not so great. Other people scorn or denigrate him, making him feel small and despised. But he doesn't seek recognition or approval. In pain or persecution, he remains humble and remembers Scripture.

We should have a healthy understanding of our smallness compared to God's greatness. But we often feel insignificant because of the way others treat us. During those times especially, we can make sense of the world by trusting God's righteousness.

Our two focus verses show how meditating on Scripture opens our eyes to the everlasting character of the righteousness of God, whose every word is true, and softens our hearts to delight in His Word, even in the midst of affliction.

Divine righteousness lasts forever; it never fails. It existed before God created our world. In all our present struggles, it sustains us through the power of the Holy Spirit. And someday Christ, the righteous judge, will return and make everything right.

In the second focus verse, trouble and anguish are personified as characters who bear down on the writer and grasp him in iron fists. Even under a heavy weight of difficulty and pain, the psalmist finds pleasure and satisfaction in God's commands. By God's grace, he considers them as delights.

Reveling in divine righteousness, the psalmist reiterates its eternal character: "The righteousness of thy testimonies is everlasting: give me understanding, and I shall live" (v. 144). The psalmist declares that the Word's righteousness is everlasting and seeks to understand it better. Increased knowledge of the Bible as the written Word brings a more abundant life. Christ as the living Word brings eternal life.

Do you try to hide from trouble and anguish, yet they hunt you down like heat-seeking missiles? Even when you fall under their onslaught, you can consider the Word your delight. Despite personal pain or public scorn, God and His words remain eternally righteous. Rejoice in that divine and everlasting righteousness!

Questions for Reflection

What things am I zealous about other than God and His Word?

How do I view myself in relation to God?

How can I, in today's troubles for others and myself, delight in divine righteousness?

24

NIGHT CRIES

Scripture Reading: Psalm 119:145–152 (Qoph)

I prevented the dawning of the morning, and cried: I hoped in thy word. Mine eyes prevent the night watches, that I might meditate in thy word.
—PSALM 119:147–148

"With chronic pain, it's always three o'clock in the morning." That memorable line jumps off the page in *Pain Patients: Traits and Treatments* by Richard A. Sternbach. Those who continually struggle with pain often feel as hopeless and isolated as if they're stuck in the empty darkness of 3:00 a.m. Time stands still during the dead of night, especially when suffering eclipses slumber. Shadows fill the mind as well as the room. Loneliness intensifies anguish. Even if you live in a house full of people, in the silent watches of the night you feel all alone.

But you are not alone in your distress. Many people experience chronic pain and insomnia. Job, who epitomizes suffering in our collective consciousness, articulated nighttime feelings of misery and hopelessness: "So am I made to possess months of vanity, and wearisome nights are appointed to me. When I lie down, I say, When shall I arise, and the night be gone? and I am full of tossings to and fro unto the dawning of the day" (Job 7:3–4).

Although the nighttime sufferer is part of a large community, few of its members are available to offer physical comfort in the wee hours of the morning. But someone who offers supreme spiritual comfort is always near. This *qoph* portion of Psalm 119 shows how the suffering psalmist cries in the night to his covenant God: "I cried with my whole heart; hear me, O LORD: I will keep thy statutes. I cried unto thee; save me, and I shall keep thy testimonies" (vv. 145–46).

Do you hear the desperation in these cries? With all his heart, the psalmist pleads in the imperative: "Hear me.... Save me." His situation is urgent; his feelings are acute. Despite his obvious anxiety, the psalmist couples each of these pleas for rescue with a commitment to obey God's Word. The verbs in his vows seem to indicate progression: the determined "I will" initially and then a more resolute "I shall."

Our focus verses show that meditating on Scripture helps the writer change his attitude. Rather than tossing and turning in growing frustration, he experiences peace. Despite his tears, God's Word inspires hope that replaces his anguish.

Perhaps distress stole his sleep, but he intentionally arises early to commune with God before his busy day or uses the quiet before sleep as premium time for uninterrupted meditation. Waking in the middle of the night may even have been his usual pattern.

Recent research indicates that people in preindustrial societies slept in two segments, commonly referred to as first sleep and second sleep. When we wake in the night, for whatever reason, we can first assure ourselves that it isn't necessarily abnormal and can then try to think of that time as a gift, given by God for uninterrupted reading of His Word and communion with Him. Instead of becoming increasingly distraught, we can, like the psalmist, embrace nighttime wakefulness with hope.

His need for hope is crucial. He is overwhelmed by some impending crisis from which he has already sought God's salvation (v. 146). He pleads for deliverance, not because he believes he deserves it, but to demonstrate God's love and justice: "Hear my voice according unto thy lovingkindness: O LORD, quicken me according to thy judgment" (v. 149).

The basis for the writer's passionate plea is God's mercy. We usually associate judgment with punishment or death, but the psalmist speaks of God's judgment as the contributing factor for reviving his life. God's divine verdict grants life to the sinner through unmerited grace. God is both merciful and just. In His great mercy He hears our prayers. In His justice He gives us life, not because we deserve it but because Christ has obtained it for us. This is the loving Lord who is near in the night watches.

Let's examine the juxtaposition of near and far in the next two verses: "They draw nigh that follow after mischief: they are far from thy law. Thou art near, O LORD; and all thy commandments are truth" (vv. 150–51). Those who persecute Christians with evil purpose are far from God's law, but are drawing near the poor psalmist. Even as the psalmist's enemies close in, however, he reminds himself of the greater reality: the covenant Lord is much closer. The Lord is near the believer who recognizes the unified truth of the Bible.

These night cries conclude with a confession of a long-held belief in the everlasting nature of the Word: "Concerning thy testimonies, I have known of old that thou hast founded them for ever" (v. 152). God established His Word before the dawn of creation. It will still stand firm when the stars fall and the sky rolls up like a scroll (Isa. 34:4; Rev. 6:14).

When you wake in the night, don't despair. Cry to the Lord. Day may seem like a dim illusion, but it will dawn. Light dispels darkness. Hope removes gloom. Peace replaces pain. God is closer to you than any persecutors. May His eternal and true Word sustain you through the dark watches of your nights.

Questions for Reflection

What concerns or aches wake me in the night, and how can I view this time differently?

In what ways is God's justice like His mercy?

In what ways can I share the hope of the Lord's nearness with others who cry in the night?

25

TENDER MERCIES

Scripture Reading: Psalm 119:153–160 (Resh)

*Great are thy tender mercies, O LORD: quicken me accord-
ing to thy judgments.*
                                                    —PSALM 119:156

How wonderful to consider the greatness of God's tender
mercies! The thought of tenderness evokes gentle feelings
and compassionate images. I envision a loving mother caring
for her precious child, who lies ill in bed. The idea of mercy
immediately brings to my mind God's favor to wretched
sinners like me. Tender mercies, indeed!

Various biblical authors mention this lovely phrase
throughout Scripture. We came across it in an earlier verse
of Psalm 119 (v. 77), and it occurs in several other psalms as
well. Psalm 25:6 links God's tender mercies with His steadfast love and describes them as "ever of old." Psalm 40:11
asks God not to hold back His tender mercies and to allow
His unfailing love and truth to continually preserve believers. David begins his penitential prayer (subsequent to his
sins involving Bathsheba and Uriah) by begging God to
blot out his transgressions according to the "multitude" of
His tender mercies (Ps. 51:1). God's "multitude" of tender

mercies is repeated in Psalm 69:16. Psalm 77:9 asks if God has forgotten to be gracious and in anger shut up His tender mercies, while Psalm 79:8 begs God to let His tender mercies "speedily" meet us, for "we are brought very low." Psalm 103:4, a familiar verse, extols the Lord as the One who redeems believers from destruction and crowns them with loving-kindness and tender mercies. God's tender mercies cover all His works (Ps. 145:9).

The phrase can be used negatively. Proverbs 12:10 contrasts the care a righteous man gives to his livestock with the "tender mercies of the wicked," which "are cruel." Jeremiah proclaims God's judgment when the Lord had removed His peace, loving-kindness, and tender mercies (Jer. 16:5).

In the New Testament, Paul longs after the Philippians in the tender mercies of Christ Jesus (Phil. 1:8). He prefaces his request for them to be likeminded by appealing to the consolation in Christ, the comfort of love, the fellowship of the Spirit, and tender mercies (Phil. 2:1). Similarly, he asks the saints at Colossae to put on "tender mercies, kindness, humility, meekness, longsuffering" while bearing with one another and forgiving one another just as Christ forgave them (Col. 3:12–13, NKJV).

What does this brief word study teach us about the phrase "tender mercies"? It is helpful first to realize that the King James Version of the New Testament texts uses the phrases "in the bowels of Jesus Christ" (Phil. 1:8); "if any bowels and mercies" (Phil. 2:1); and "bowels of mercy" (Col. 3:12). This language sounds strange—perhaps vulgar or indelicate—to modern ears, but the archaic meaning of "bowels" as the seat of emotions helps us comprehend the deepness of this feeling.

God faithfully pours out blessings on believers and on all creation (Ps. 145:9) throughout history as crowning expressions of His deep love and gentle kindness. The proverb about caring for livestock seems to add provision and sustenance, elements of God's sovereign providence. The cruelty of the wicked farmer reflects a failure to acknowledge that everything he has comes from God's merciful hand. Jeremiah shows that God's judgment includes the removal of His blessings.

The unbeliever doesn't rejoice in God's tender mercies because he doesn't have them or even know of them. If you came to faith later in life, you may remember a previous lack of peace and joy. What you needed were the tender mercies of Christ Jesus (Phil. 1:8). His Spirit brings peace to our hearts and to our congregations (Phil. 2:1). His forgiveness enables us to forgive others while clothing ourselves in kindness, humility, meekness, longsuffering, and tender mercies (Col. 3:12).

This stanza of Psalm 119 reiterates concepts we have seen in recent stanzas. It begins with a plea and a familiar vow: "Consider mine affliction, and deliver me: for I do not forget thy law" (v. 153). The psalmist's prayer for deliverance from affliction is once more coupled with confession. As we've seen in previous stanzas and see frequently in this one, the psalmist equates deliverance with life: "Plead my cause, and deliver me: quicken me according to thy word" (v. 154). Doesn't this verse remind you of Christ's work? He intercedes for us at God's right hand (Rom. 8:34), redeems us through His blood (Eph. 1:7; Col. 1:14), and revives us by granting us a new life (Rom. 6:4)—all in fulfillment of biblical promises. That redemption is not near those who reject

God's Word and Spirit: "Salvation is far from the wicked: for they seek not thy statutes" (v. 155). The focus verse, then, reminds us of God's deep love and abundant mercy toward those brought to new life according to God's promise.

Although surrounded by adversaries, the psalmist doesn't swerve from the Word: "Many are my persecutors and mine enemies; yet do I not decline from thy testimonies" (v. 157). As we've seen before, he loves God's law and hates to see it broken: "I beheld the transgressors, and was grieved; because they kept not thy word" (v. 158). Other versions indicate that seeing disregard for God's law sickens the psalmist's heart to the point of disgust.

The psalmist began this section by asking God to reflect on his affliction, and now he asks God to think about his delight: "Consider how I love thy precepts: quicken me, O LORD, according to thy lovingkindness" (v. 159). This is the stanza's third request for God to revive the psalmist. These pleas have been made in accordance with God's Word, His judgments, and now His loving-kindness, which is God's love and care within the covenantal relationship.

Believers love God because God loves believers (1 John 4:19). But our relationship with God far surpasses that with any human. God's love is unfailing and His promises are true. The psalmist says, "Thy word is true from the beginning: and every one of thy righteous judgments endureth for ever" (v. 160). The sum of God's Word is truth. The Bible is a cohesive unit of which every precept lasts forever.

This stanza of Psalm 119 reinforces the truths we've heard while stressing God's deep love and gentle grace. May God open your eyes to His tender mercies in your life.

Questions for Reflection

How has looking at references to "tender mercies" increased my appreciation for God's care?

In what areas might I be failing to demonstrate my new life?

In what ways can I express tender mercies to others today?

26

GREAT PEACE

Scripture Reading: Psalm 119:161–168 (Sin and Shin)

Great peace have they which love thy law: and nothing shall offend them.
—PSALM 119:165

As we near the end of Psalm 119, familiar themes form a lattice, supporting the blooming rose of peace. The blossoms emit fragrances of awe, joy, hope, and praise for God's great salvation.

In the first verse, the psalmist's often-expressed love for the Word rises to awe: "Princes have persecuted me without a cause: but my heart standeth in awe of thy word" (v. 161). When political or ecclesiastical leaders wrong us without reason, we can dispel vengeance, bitterness, or despair by filling our hearts and minds with awe for God and His Word. Exploring God's written and natural revelations—the Bible and creation—generates praise to the One who deserves all glory and honor.

Our awe-filled joy can be as exultant as the soldier who, in the midst of battle, discovers a beautiful golden goblet encrusted with priceless gems: "I rejoice at thy word, as one that findeth great spoil" (v. 162). Such triumphant joy comes from loving God's Word. Love for God's truths leads to hate for the world's lies: "I hate and abhor lying: but thy law do I love" (v. 163).

God's truth grounds our perspective and emotions in a world filled with deceit. Falsehood is so much a part of our culture that we expect it from most politicians and the media. But its prevalence shouldn't lull us into unquestioningly accepting it. God calls us not merely to tolerate or dislike lying, but to hate and abhor it. If you love God's law, you immerse yourself in its truth. And if you love God, you love to pray. The psalmist sets an example: "Seven times a day do I praise thee because of thy righteous judgments" (v. 164). Jewish believers went to the temple three times daily for prayer, but the psalmist prays more than twice that much. How often do you pray each day? Maybe you get up early for a quiet time with God or pray before you fall asleep at night. (Can you stay awake until "amen"?) Perhaps you ask a blessing before you eat. Many families have a great tradition of Scripture reading and prayer at meal times.

You may be patting yourself on the back right now because you've developed an attitude of prayer. All day you pray without ceasing (1 Thess. 5:17). But think about the specifics of your thoughts. Do you punch out prayers like pushing buttons on a vending machine: "Give me this" or "Give me that"? Do you whine like a demanding toddler?

Psalm 119's prayer has been replete with pleas for blessing or assistance, but now we see its praise and peace. Seven is the biblical number signifying completeness or fullness. The psalmist's comprehensive daily praise generates great peace.

The "great peace" in our focus verse is the Hebrew word *shalom*. Far more than a simple absence of conflict, *shalom* encompasses a complex meaning that includes completeness and calmness, health and wholeness, safety and prosperity, tranquility and harmony, as well as security and rest in the Lord. This is the comfort of God's covenant care for His people. Unbelievers do not experience this deep inner peace, but all who love God's law have it. We still struggle with sin and adversity, but no thing or person can cause permanent offense or make us stumble irretrievably. Our peace and salvation are secure: "LORD, I have hoped for thy salvation, and done thy commandments. My soul hath kept thy testimonies; and I love them exceedingly" (vv. 166–67).

Believers can hope for earthly rescue and be assured of eternal salvation. Out of gratitude for Christ's redemption, we obey God's commands in love. God the Father grants us *hope* through His free gift of salvation, we live in *hope-filled* love through the Spirit, and we *hopefully* look to Christ's return and the fulfillment of His kingdom. With our innermost soul and every fiber of our being, we love and live for our triune God.

While living in hopeful obedience and enthusiastic love, we know that God sees everything we do and each event that happens to us. "I have kept thy precepts and thy testimonies: for all my ways are before thee" (v. 168). God sees all our actions and knows every inclination of our hearts. No sin can be hidden from Him. True believers don't hide personal agendas behind a smokescreen of feigned humility and hypocritical piety. They are genuinely humble, realizing that God sees and knows all.

The fragrant rose of God's *shalom* thrives on the framework of loving God's law. Our daily prayers—spontaneous or structured—can ascend in a pleasant aroma filled with awe for the Creator God and Savior Christ, joy at the beauty and value of the Word, hope for the present as well as the future, and praise for God's providential care. An experiential awareness of God's great peace helps us genuinely love Him and others.

May God fill your heart with His *shalom* as we pray for the peace of our local congregations and Christ's church throughout the world.

Questions for Reflection

How might my perception of God be lacking in awe or joy?

In what ways do I keep myself from experiencing the fullness of God's *shalom*?

How can I conform both internally and externally to the command to love God and others today?

27

PROCLAIMED PRAISE

Scripture Reading: Psalm 119:169–176 (Taw)

My lips shall utter praise, when thou hast taught me thy statutes. My tongue shall speak of thy word: for all thy commandments are righteousness.
—PSALM 119:171–172

Our stanza-by-stanza study has demonstrated how this long psalm is far more than an intricately constructed ode that extols God's law. It's an emotive prayer of the believer struggling to live an obedient life in a broken world. And it's a practical manual for discovering delight despite suffering. While focusing on God and His Word, it consistently points us to the living Word, Jesus Christ.

Just as the book of Psalms as a whole moves from primarily lament to predominately praise, Psalm 119 crescendos to this final climax of exaltation. The first two verses of this stanza parallel each other as the psalmist cries out, "Let my cry come before thee, O LORD: give me understanding according to thy word. Let my supplication come before thee: deliver me according to thy word" (vv. 169–170). Notice the psalmist's priority: he first pleads for the Lord to hear his cry in order that he may have understanding. His request for deliverance comes second. What good is it to be delivered from trouble if we lack biblical understanding? Both requests are made according to God's Word. The psalmist seeks God's will, not his own.

Our focus verses, stressing vocal praise, appear next. Like the previous verses, they parallel each other. The first phrase of each describes a physical feature—the lips or the tongue—proclaiming praise. The second phrases acknowledge our dependence on God and the righteousness of His Word. Because God teaches us His Word and because all His commandments are right, we are called to pour forth praise. This praise should flow from us not only in thoughts and prayers but also in speech and song.

The next verse shows a familiar combination: a plea for assistance and a confession of personal godliness: "Let thine hand help me; for I have chosen thy precepts" (v. 173). We often hear or say that what happens in your life isn't as important as how you respond. We have little choice about many life-changing events, but we can choose to follow biblical precepts in our reaction to them. More than that, we can decide to delight: "I have longed for thy salvation, O LORD; and thy law is my delight" (v. 174).

Perhaps you're thinking, "I can't simply decide to delight. Joy is an emotion, not a decision." While it's true that joy is an emotion, we can't argue with this psalm's clear teaching about loving God's law and delighting in it. Psalm 119:16 showed the psalmist making a determination: "I *will* delight." We can commit to loving God's Word and delighting in it. We may not always experience a feeling of happiness—we have often seen the psalmist's great distress—but believers have a deep-seated delight that transcends volatile feelings. This deep-rooted joy is based on the written and living Word.

Like the psalmist, we long for God's salvation, but unlike him we have seen Jesus in the pages of Scripture. The psalmist looked for the coming Messiah, but we anticipate His return. Knowing that He has already accomplished our salvation, we have assurance that He will renew our bodies and the world.

As we look to the Lord and lean on Him during life's trials, we grow to love and obey His Word with increasing joy. As we exercise our commitment, delight permeates our entire being and overflows in praise. We can pray with confidence like the psalmist: "Let my soul live, and it shall praise thee; and let thy judgments help me" (v. 175).

My soul has been redeemed from eternal death to a new life in Christ. Shouldn't I praise God with all that is within me (Ps. 103:1)? Shouldn't I praise the One from whom my help comes, the Maker of heaven and earth (Ps. 121:2)?

This psalm began with a benediction for those who walk in the law of the Lord (v. 1) and has shown us the path of faithful obedience. Along the way, the psalmist has often maintained his innocence, but he concludes by admitting his sin: "I have gone astray like a lost sheep; seek thy servant; for I do not forget thy commandments" (v. 176).

We have seen a lot of railing against the wicked in this psalm, so it is instructive that it ends with a confession of personal sin. Recognition of our own guilt should shape our attitude when we've been injured. It is crucial to recognize our own proclivity to sin as well as our capacity to hurt others. Who among us doesn't have a tendency to use others for selfish purposes or personal gain?

The author couches his repentant confession in shepherding imagery. He admits he has left the path like a wayward sheep. Isaiah uses similar language in a corporate confession as he prophesies with amazing accuracy about the coming Christ: "All we like sheep have gone astray; we have turned every one to his own way; and the LORD hath laid on him the iniquity of us all" (Isa. 53:6).

Jesus Christ bore our iniquity. He called Himself the Good Shepherd (John 1:11, 14). We are all sinners who stray from the flock and need the supreme Shepherd to find us and return us to the fold. When the psalmist admits to wandering like a lost sheep, he asks God to seek him. Doesn't this remind us of Christ's parable about the lost sheep (Matt. 18:10–14; Luke 15:1–7)? The psalmist concludes his prayer with personal repentance that points forward to Christ, the living Word.

This carefully crafted poem shows us it is not enough simply to know God's Word; we must obey it and delight in it. And we cannot do either apart from a personal relationship with Jesus Christ, the Word made flesh.

I pray that this survey has opened your eyes to the beauty of God's longest poem and filled your heart with joy. May your delight pour out in proclaimed praise!

Questions for Reflection

How can I seek understanding prior to begging for deliverance?

In what specific ways can I decide to delight?

Why should I consider my own sin when others have hurt me?

28

RIDE HIGH

Scripture Reading: Isaiah 58

*Then shalt thou delight thyself in the LORD; and I will
cause thee to ride upon the high places of the earth, and feed
thee with the heritage of Jacob thy father: for the mouth of the
LORD hath spoken it.*
—ISAIAH 58:14

Isaiah 58 is a powerful speech from the Lord that contrasts feigned and real delight, false and true worship, and
artificial and authentic righteousness. God begins by com-
manding Isaiah to "cry aloud" and lift up his voice "like
a trumpet" to confront God's people with their transgressions and sins (v. 1).

Why? Because these sinful people are only acting religious and pious: "Yet they seek me daily, and delight to know
my ways, as a nation that did righteousness, and forsook not
the ordinance of their God: they ask of me the ordinances of
justice; they take delight in approaching to God" (Isa. 58:2).
They put on a pretentious show, coming to the temple every
day, seemingly thrilled to learn all about God. They practice
a pious nationalism that consists of religious form, arrogantly presuming they would never abandon God's ways.

Pretending to delight in worship, they think only of self, asking God for His justice on their behalf.

The next verses become increasingly convicting. God initially addresses their complaint that He hasn't noticed their fasting and self-sacrifice. He points out that they fast only to please themselves. Despite the religious practice of denying themselves food, they continue to indulge in sinful behaviors. They oppress their workers, bicker with each other, and strike with wicked fists. God does not approve of their vain fasting, which accomplishes nothing except impeding their prayers (vv. 3–4).

He asks a series of questions that causes readers to consider ways we render religious practice meaningless by our failures to express God's love:

> Is it such a fast that I have chosen? a day for a man to afflict his soul? is it to bow down his head as a bulrush, and to spread sackcloth and ashes under him? wilt thou call this a fast, and an acceptable day to the LORD?
>
> Is not this the fast that I have chosen? to loose the bands of wickedness, to undo the heavy burdens, and to let the oppressed go free, and that ye break every yoke? Is it not to deal thy bread to the hungry, and that thou bring the poor that are cast out to thy house? when thou seest the naked, that thou cover him: and that thou hide not thyself from thine own flesh? (vv. 5–7)

One can hardly get more practical than this! These people pretend to be humble by bowing like reeds bent in the wind, covering themselves with sackcloth, and kneeling in ashes. God doesn't accept that kind of external piety. He prefers to see "fasting" that consists of compassionate actions: freeing those who have been unjustly imprisoned

and lightening the load of overworked employees, setting
free the oppressed and breaking the chains from the bound,
sharing food with the hungry, providing shelter and clothing
for the homeless. The conclusion is particularly convicting:
We must make time to help our own relatives with a willing
attitude rather than ignoring or avoiding them.

If we demonstrate our authentic faith through such
actions, God will bless us: "Then shall thy light break forth
as the morning, and thine health shall spring forth speedily: and thy righteousness shall go before thee; the glory of
the LORD shall be thy rearward" (v. 8). The light of our
salvation will brighten like dawn, and our healing will soar.
Godliness propels us forward, while God's glory surrounds
and crowns us. Hypocrisy vanishes and humility appears.
Then the Lord answers us quickly.

> Then shalt thou call, and the LORD shall answer; thou
> shalt cry, and he shall say, Here I am. If thou take away
> from the midst of thee the yoke, the putting forth of the
> finger, and speaking vanity; and if thou draw out thy soul
> to the hungry, and satisfy the afflicted soul; then shall thy
> light rise in obscurity, and thy darkness be as the noon
> day: and the LORD shall guide thee continually, and sat-
> isfy thy soul in drought, and make fat thy bones: and thou
> shalt be like a watered garden, and like a spring of water,
> whose waters fail not. (vv. 9–11)

We must stop oppressing others with heavy burdens,
pointing fingers, spreading rumors, or speaking arrogantly.
We should pour ourselves into feeding the hungry and
helping troubled souls. If we do these things, the light of
Christ will shine in our darkness and make it as bright as
midday. God will guide us; He will satisfy our souls and

increase our strength until we feel like a verdant garden and a perpetual fountain.

God's people are called to be builders: "And they that shall be of thee shall build the old waste places: thou shalt raise up the foundations of many generations; and thou shalt be called, The repairer of the breach, The restorer of paths to dwell in" (v. 12). We are to edify rather than tear down. Ruins need to be rebuilt and foundations need to be laid for coming generations. We must mend wrecked fences and restore broken homes. The believer who works toward renewal will be called Repairer and Restorer.

We also need to practice true religion: "If thou turn away thy foot from the sabbath, from doing thy pleasure on my holy day; and call the sabbath a delight, the holy of the LORD, honourable; and shalt honour him, not doing thine own ways, nor finding thine own pleasure, nor speaking thine own words" (v. 13).

Like fasting, keeping the Sabbath holy involves more than the appearance of piety. True observance of the day arises from a heart that desires to do God's will rather than pleasing self and pursuing personal interests. We properly delight in Sunday when we view it as God's holy day instead of as a day off that we can use for ourselves. When we seek to honor Him in all we do on Sunday—and every day— we will long less for our own pleasures and talk less about ourselves. Sabbath observance is only one aspect of this chapter's practical application about practicing true religion.

Our focus verse assures us that if we replace feigned religiosity with real righteousness, we will delight in the Lord. God promises to honor us by causing us to ride in high places. He will satisfy us with our covenant heritage.

He has spoken this, and it is sure to be. Ride high on God's certain promise!

Questions for Reflection

In what ways might my religious practices be a false front?

How do I negate my witness to others by failing to show God's love?

What can I do today to show God and others that my faith is genuine?

29

WORD FEAST

Scripture Reading: Jeremiah 15

Thy words were found, and I did eat them; and thy word was unto me the joy and rejoicing of mine heart: for I am called by thy name, O LORD God of hosts.

—JEREMIAH 15:16

Amid Jeremiah's depressing pronouncements of God's judgment, the prophet feasts on God's words, and we share a taste of his joy. God's Word piques the heart's appetite and satisfies the soul like a bountiful banquet.

The first verses of Jeremiah 15 relate—in frighteningly descriptive language—God's judgment against the people of Judah, who had forsaken Him: "Thou hast forsaken me, saith the LORD, thou art gone backward: therefore will I stretch out my hand against thee, and destroy thee; I am weary with repenting (v. 6).

The Lord was wearied with the people's repenting because it was not genuine or lasting. As soon as they begged God for forgiveness, they descended again into the same sins. Real repentance is more than merely saying, "I'm sorry" (especially, "I'm sorry, but..."). It is far more than feeling remorse over getting caught. It is easy to express penitence but difficult to keep from falling into familiar and cherished sins. True repentance is deep sorrow and conviction of personal sin accompanied by strong commitment and an effort to overcome the sin. It is a changed heart, corroborated by changed actions. Paul speaks of "godly sorrow" that leads to repentance (2 Cor. 7:9–10). Lord's Day 30 of the Heidelberg Catechism describes genuine repentance as the "dying-away of the old self, and the coming-to-life of the new" (A. 88). It defines this "dying-away" as "to be genuinely sorry for sin, to hate it more and more, and to run away from it" (A. 89). The people in Jeremiah's day didn't run from sin; they embraced it.

In this chapter's dialogue between God and Jeremiah, we learn that the people had cursed Jeremiah for proclaiming God's judgments, and he feels overwhelmed (v. 10). But God has a word of assurance: "The LORD said, Verily it shall be well with thy remnant; verily I will cause the enemy to entreat thee well in the time of evil and in the time of affliction" (v. 11). Despite the coming wrath upon the nation, God would see to Jeremiah's personal welfare and preserve for Himself a faithful remnant. He controls everything—even enemies and exile. He can make our worst enemy treat us well, if that serves His purpose.

God goes on to decree that enemies would overcome Judah, plundering its wealth and carrying its people into exile (vv. 12–14). In Jeremiah's response to this dismal prediction, he asks God to avenge his persecution and remove his suffering, which he underwent for the Lord's sake (v. 15).

In our focus verse, Jeremiah describes his discovery and consumption of God's words as finding and enjoying a wonderful feast. He didn't merely taste the words, he ate them. Jeremiah took God's Word into himself as deeply as ingesting food. He chewed on it. He digested it. He assimilated the words to his soul as a body utilizes food to nourish its cells. God's Word delighted him in the depths of his heart. He emphasizes this gladness with doubled terms, speaking of the "joy and rejoicing" of his heart. He exults because he was called by the God of Hosts and is known by His name.

Like Jeremiah, Ezekiel ate the Word. God told Ezekiel, who prophesied God's judgment to Judah's sister nation, Israel, to eat the scroll containing God's words, which were sweet as honey (2:8–9; 3:1–3). Both of these scenes are similar to when John eats the scroll that makes his belly bitter, but tastes sweet as honey (Rev. 10:9–10).

Jeremiah, Ezekiel, and John were messengers who delighted in the sweetness of the Word, but bitterly grieved the suffering they prophesied. Christians delight in the Word, but often face persecution because of it. While God's Word is sweet to believers, it can be bitter to unbelievers because sometimes the truth hurts.

Jeremiah continues his speech with a phrase reminiscent of Psalm 1:1. He says, "I sat not in the assembly of the mockers, nor rejoiced; I sat alone because of thy hand: for thou hast filled me with indignation" (v. 17). Jeremiah has not joined in mockery or revelry, choosing isolation rather than camaraderie with the disobedient and unrepentant. His anger is righteous, directed against the breaking of God's law.

He concludes with questions that could reflect his human frailty and Judah's unfaithfulness, but which he may have asked rhetorically, in faith: Will the pain be perpetual and the wound incurable? Will God seem a liar or like waters that fail (v. 18)? We know that God will provide eventual relief, even from lifelong pain. We trust God, who is not a man that He should lie (Num. 23:19). The source of living fountains of water (Rev. 7:17) will never vanish like a dry stream or disappear like a desert mirage.

God answers Jeremiah's questionable queries with His faithful promises:

> Therefore thus saith the LORD, if thou return, then will I bring thee again, and thou shalt stand before me: and if thou take forth the precious from the vile, thou shalt be as my mouth: let them return unto thee; but return not thou unto them. And I will make thee unto this people a fenced brazen wall: and they shall fight against thee, but they shall not prevail against thee: for I am with thee to save thee and to deliver thee, saith the LORD.
>
> And I will deliver thee out of the hand of the wicked, and I will redeem thee out of the hand of the terrible. (vv. 19–21)

This message specifically encouraged Jeremiah to remain faithful and continue calling the people to return to the Lord. God would strengthen him and deliver him. But these promises are also for all believers. If those who stray return to God's ways, the Lord will restore them to His presence. If they choose righteous behavior rather than vile actions, they witness for God. If they give up relationships that weaken their faith and instead seek fellowship with other believers, they will become strong. They may fall into the hands of the wicked, but even then they can look with joy to their deliverance—if not in this life, then when God takes them to their heavenly home.

Through all God's bitter providences, cling to His sweet promises. Feast on them!

Questions for Reflection

What aspects of my repentance lack genuineness?

Am I merely tasting or joyfully digesting God's Word?

In what specific ways today can I let go of the bitter and embrace the sweet?

DEEP DELIGHT

30

Scripture Reading: Romans 7

For I delight in the law of God after the inward man.
—ROMANS 7:22

This penultimate meditation in our study answers its ultimate question: How can I love God's law? We've explored twenty-nine texts about delighting in God's Word, so we know it is something all Christians should do. But how does one go about doing that? How do we translate theoretical knowledge or even experiential feeling into practical action? Romans 7 reveals the answer: through Christ.

God enables all people to live and move and have their being (Acts 17:28). We can't think or feel or do anything on our own. And we cannot delight in God's law unless Jesus lives in our hearts.

This chapter of Paul's letter to the Romans examines the place of the law in the Christian's life. Paul explains how through Christ we are no longer bound to the law (vv. 1–6), how the law makes us conscious of our sin (vv. 7–13), and finally how redeemed saints still struggle with temptation (vv. 14–25).

He begins with an analogy of marriage. Marriage vows are binding only as long as both spouses live (vv. 1–2). A person is free to marry again after the death of a husband or wife (v. 3). Similarly, after our sinful nature died with Christ on the cross, we are freed from the power of the law and joined to the One who was raised from the dead: "Wherefore, my brethren, ye also are become dead to the law by the body of Christ; that ye should be married to another, even to him who is raised from the dead, that we should bring forth fruit unto God" (v. 4). Due to this union with Christ, the believer produces good fruit to God's glory. But for those still controlled by the old nature, the law arouses sinful desires that yield a harvest of rotten fruit, which evidences the dead wood in the tree's core (v. 5).

Released from the bonds of sin's law, Christians can serve God with a new nature that follows the spirit, rather than the letter, of the law: "But now we are delivered from the law, that being dead wherein we were held; that we should serve in newness of spirit, and not in the oldness of the letter" (v. 6).

Lest his readers should get the idea that the law is bad and ought to be discarded, Paul emphatically clarifies how the law functions in making Christians conscious of sin. "What shall we say then? Is the law sin? God forbid," says Paul, "Nay, I had not known sin, but by the law: for I had not known lust, except the law had said, Thou shalt not covet" (v. 7). The law shows us our sin. Paul highlights the tenth commandment because it applies to every other one. The Heidelberg Catechism meaningfully explains the implications of this commandment:

Q. 113: What is God's will for us in the tenth commandment?

A.: That not even the slightest thought or desire contrary to any one of God's commandments should ever arise in my heart. Rather, with all my heart I should always hate sin and take pleasure in whatever is right.

Coveting demonstrates a heart filled with desires that are contrary to God's commandments. We must squelch even the most niggling thought or slightest desire against any of God's laws that rears its ugly head in our hearts. Instead, we should wholeheartedly hate sin and delight in what is right.

Paul relates how sin seized opportunity through the commandment to generate all kinds of covetousness within him (v. 8). He had once been secure in his own righteousness, with no conviction of sin. When he realized the extent of his sinfulness, that self-righteous person died (v. 9). Though the purpose of the law is to bring life, it is a death sentence to the person who tries to earn salvation. But the law is not the problem; it is sin that deceives. The law itself is holy, righteous, and good (vv. 10–12). Paul stresses it was not the law, but sin that brought death to him (v. 13).

He then reflects on the Christian's continual struggle to live a godly life. Sin no longer controls us, but we are still sinners (v. 14). We find ourselves doing the bad things we don't want to do. And we fail to do the good things we want to do (v. 15). This continuing conflict demonstrates that the Christian recognizes the law as good (v. 16), yet the sin that remains in us keeps us from doing the good we would like to do (vv. 17–21).

Our focus verse shows that in our innermost being, we delight in the law of God. We love our heavenly Father and want to honor Him by being obedient children. But our weak flesh keeps succumbing to temptation and makes us prisoners of sin (v. 23). Conflicted Paul cries, "O wretched man that I am! who shall deliver me from the body of this death?" (v. 24). The answer resounds down through the ages: "I thank God through Jesus Christ our Lord. So then with the mind I myself serve the law of God; but with the flesh the law of sin" (v. 25).

Paul summarizes what he has been saying: His inner being loves and serves the law of God, but the vestiges of his sinful nature often cause him to fall into sin. It seems hopeless. The battle, however, does not belong to us. The victory belongs to Jesus Christ, who has fully paid for all our sins and freed us from eternal condemnation.

Only by trusting in the finished work of Christ, with an awareness of our own sinful tendencies, can we experience true delight in God's Word and live for Him.

Questions for Reflection

How has looking carefully at Romans 7 changed my view of the law?

What specific strategies can I use to stop doing some of the things I really don't want to do?

In what ways can I demonstrate my delight in God's law to others today?

31

VICTORIOUS WORD

Scripture Reading: Revelation 19

His name is called The Word of God.
—REVELATION 19:13

Revelation 19 swells with dynamic scenes and sounds, celebrating the military triumph and marriage supper of King Jesus, our victorious Lord and God's living Word. The apostle John, exiled for his faith to the island of Patmos, experienced and recorded these multisensory visions.

Chapter 18 described the fall of Babylon, which represents the wicked seduction of the world. Verse 20 of that chapter called on the hosts of heaven and the apostles and prophets to rejoice over her destruction. Chapter 19 begins with the response. John hears the loud shout of a multitude in heaven praising God: "Alleluia; Salvation, and glory, and honour, and power, unto the Lord our God: For true and righteous are his judgments" (vv. 1–2). This multitude extols God's righteous judgment in destroying the forces of evil and avenging His people. The twenty-four elders and four living creatures worship with the throng, prostrating themselves before God's throne and crying, "Amen; Alleluia"

(Rev. 19:4). The elders represent the entire church, possibly the twelve tribes of the old covenant and the twelve apostles of the new. Commentators' interpretations of the four living creatures vary, but the beings' close proximity to the throne and their six wings seem to represent a high order of angelic messengers. They worship God intimately and serve Him swiftly. The similarities between these creatures and those described by Ezekiel in chapters 1 and 10 seem to confirm that they represent exalted angels.

John's vision continues, and he hears a single mighty voice near the throne command: "Praise our God, all ye his servants, and ye that fear him, both great and small" (v. 5). Spectacle and sound increase when, like the roar of a mighty cataract, a vast host proclaims: "Alleluia: for the Lord God omnipotent reigneth" (v. 6). Doesn't this fill your mind with that stirring climax of Handel's *Messiah*, the "Hallelujah Chorus"?

Did you realize that thrilling and thunderous proclamation is a prelude for the ultimate wedding ceremony? "Let us be glad and rejoice, and give honour to him: for the marriage of the Lamb is come, and his wife hath made herself ready" (v. 7). The Bible frequently uses a wedding analogy to describe the relationship between Christ and His church.

We can better understand the use of the imagery in this context when we consider how marriages differed in ancient Jewish culture. Betrothal was more than a mere engagement; it included some elements of modern weddings. In the presence of witnesses, the betrothed parties agreed to the marriage terms, and God's blessing was pronounced upon the couple. They legally became husband and wife, although they did not yet live together. If the groom still had to pay a dowry to the bride's father, he did that during a subsequent interval. Near its end, the bride prepared herself at her family home. The groom dressed in his best and led his friends, singing and carrying lights, to the bride's house. After he received his betrothed, the entire procession returned to his home. The grand finale was the wedding feast, which could last a week or more.

Do you see how the ancient custom mirrors the church's relationship with Christ? God chose the bride before time began. During the Old Testament period, the wedding was announced. In the New Testament time frame, God became man, and the betrothal took place. God paid the dowry in full on the cross. We now live in the interval before the marriage feast, which is often described as the "already, but not yet" of church history. The church is already the bride of Christ, but it does not yet enjoy the fullness of that relationship with Him. While the church waits for Christ to come and claim her, she prepares herself like a bride getting ready for her wedding: "And to her was granted that she should be arrayed in fine linen, clean and white: for the fine linen is the righteousness of saints" (vv. 7–8). Here the church is portrayed as a bride arrayed in spotless linen, representing perfect purity. Redeemed sinners became righteous saints through the great exchange when Christ took their sin upon Himself and gave them His own righteousness. When they appear at the marriage feast of the Lamb, all the stains of sin that cling to them in this life will have been removed.

A bride in white is easy for our modern minds to imagine, and who doesn't love a romance with a happy ending? But the most touching love story on earth only faintly conveys the delight between Christ and His bride, the church.

That joy will be complete when Jesus returns. Then all true Christians will celebrate the great marriage supper of the Lamb and live with Him forever in perfect fellowship.

The believer's anticipated blessing is sure. The angel who has been guiding John through this unfolding vision tells him: "Write, Blessed are they which are called unto the marriage supper of the Lamb." Then he adds, "These are the true sayings of God" (v. 9).

Overcome with rapture and awe, John falls at this angel's feet, but is admonished to worship only God, not a fellow servant (v. 10).

Then it is as if heaven itself splits open and the royal Bridegroom rides forth. This scene reminds us of verses about the sun we read in an earlier meditation:

> Their line is gone out through all the earth, and their words to the end of the world. In them hath he set a tabernacle for the sun, which is as a bridegroom coming out of his chamber, and rejoiceth as a strong man to run a race. His going forth is from the end of the heaven, and his circuit unto the ends of it: and there is nothing hid from the heat thereof. (Ps. 19:4–6)

The sun's glory is a dim reflection of the Son's glory. Revelation 19's description should decisively dispel any misconceptions about Jesus as being merely meek and mild. He certainly is humble and compassionate, but He is also awesome and mighty:

> And I saw heaven opened, and behold a white horse; and he that sat upon him was called Faithful and True, and in righteousness he doth judge and make war. His eyes were as a flame of fire, and on his head were many crowns; and he had a name written, that no man knew, but he himself.

And he was clothed with a vesture dipped in blood: and
his name is called The Word of God. (vv. 11–13)

Christ is the living and breathing Word of God; He is
Faithful and True; His flaming eyes see all. Crowned with
incomparable majesty, He is the definitive victor. Yet mys-
tery remains; a name is written that He alone knows. But
anyone can read His written revelation. Jesus is the victorious Word we love and in whom we delight.

Following in His magnificent wake are the armies of
heaven, seated on white horses and clothed in clean linen
(v. 14). The Word of God takes action:

> And out of his mouth goeth a sharp sword, that with it he
> should smite the nations: and he shall rule them with a rod
> of iron: and he treadeth the winepress of the fierceness and
> wrath of Almighty God.
>
> And he hath on his vesture and on his thigh a name
> written, *KING OF KINGS, AND LORD OF LORDS.*
> (vv. 15–16)

What a picture of the conquering Christ, our supreme
King and highest Lord! He comes to destroy all who have
fought against God and persecuted His church. Their
destruction is so certain that before a battle even takes place
an angel in the sun calls the birds to feast on the carcasses
(vv. 17–18).

This final battle doesn't last long. All the anti-Christian
forces of the world gather for war, but the beast and false
prophet are immediately captured and cast into the fiery
lake (vv. 19, 20). The beast represents Satan's persecuting
power and the false prophet represents his deceiving power.
At Christ's return, every scheme of Satan to persecute and
deceive will be confined eternally in hell. The summons of

the angel in the sun is fulfilled as the sword of the Lord annihilates all God's enemies forever (v. 21).

These meditations have progressively shown what it means to love God's law and delight in it while we love and delight in Christ, the victorious Word. As we conclude these meditations, my prayer for you is a Trinitarian benediction based on Romans 15:13, "Now the God of hope fill you with all joy and peace in believing, that ye may abound in hope, through the power of the Holy Ghost."

Questions for Reflection

In what ways can I live more intimately with God and serve Him more swiftly?

How can I prepare to meet my victorious King?

In what specific ways today and every day can I delight more in God's written and living Word?